Praise

Courage Doesn't Always Roar

"Finally, the business book we all need has been written by Mary Anne Radmacher. Her insight, wisdom and ability to get leaders to look within and reflect is invaluable. *Courage Doesn't Always Roar* is another tool to share with my team and fellow CEOs as we navigate leadership and authenticity together. Her words create a common language and inspire thought leadership. I have shared Em's writings near and far and often use them when it is my turn to facilitate my Monday morning CEO call. On a personal level, I start every day with a reflection of Em's words that I keep close at hand. I find continuous reinforcement of her words and mantras that enrich and guide me. It is like visiting with a friend again and again and again when I read her pages. Em's writing style creates the ability for the reader to open her work to any page and soak it in immediately."
—Christopher K. M. Leach, CEO

" 'Courage doesn't always roar...' is one of Mary Anne Em Radmacher's most recognized aphorisms. *Courage Doesn't Always Roar: Sometimes it Does* is an invitation to explore how courage shows up in our everyday lives. It is a perfect daily inspiration book with each concept numbered and most fitting on a single page. Easy to pick up and read first thing each morning or in the 'found moments' of a busy day. The writing offers ideas that involve courage, broaden our understanding of ourselves and others, and create the potential for a more satisfying life. Each writing ends with a thought-provoking question to ponder in our days and 'enCOURAGE' us. A favorite of mine: 'Of what might you dare to dream today?' My answer 'Even more now that I have read this book!' "

—Caren Albers, author of *Happiness Junkie* and *Married to a Vegan* (memoirs) and *Homecoming: Belonging and Knowing* (poems & essays)

"Learning from Mary Anne is the gift that keeps on giving. Like many people, my first exposure to Mary Anne was her famous quotation 'Courage doesn't always roar. Sometimes courage is the quiet voice at the end of the day saying, *I will try again tomorrow.*' Mary Anne calls this a poem. I call it wisdom. Now, she has written this book about courage, the Preface of which says 'Courage deserves a wider brushstroke of understanding.' Not only am I still learning what this simple poem means, but in this book, Mary Anne continues to teach us all what else it means to be courageous. Over the years, I have collected Mary Anne's artwork and posters about courage, as well as given them as gifts to others. Now, I will give this book of Mary Anne's courageous wisdom to others as well."

—Arthur Bushkin, chairman of the Kindness Cloud Foundation

"There are those humans among us who see deeply into life, with all its magic, uncertainty, pain and bliss. These are the seers, bound to feel things at a deeper level and with more insight, and finding and illuminating patterns for the rest of us. Mary Anne Em Radmacher is such a seer, using words and images and color to help all of us see more deeply, feel more strongly, and understand more fully our own responsibilities to be courageous, to own and explore our feelings but not let them trap us. Read this book for a master class in being fully and unapologetically human."

—Patti Digh, author of *Life is a Verb* and *Geography of Loss*

"Reassuring. Engaging. Uplifting. Mary Anne has done it again! This book delightfully captures the essence of her informed wisdom, unique writing style, and quirky humor. Beyond the useful ideas that reliably address some of life's many conundrums, each chapter concludes with a question that invites reflection, direction, and action. Like courage itself, this book sometimes whispers...and at other times it roars. Get ready to listen and respond!"

—Paul Wesselmann, the Ripples Guy (writer, speaker, adventurer)

"Wise. Warm. Infused with strength easily inhaled. Once again the creative spirit of Mary Anne Radmacher is a gift to all who seek courage for both the hard things and the everyday. May readers find what they need in *Courage Doesn't Always Roar*, a wisdom book carrying words to help each of us "try again tomorrow."

—Jane Kirkpatrick, NYTimes bestselling author of
  The Healing of Natalie Curtis

"[This book] came to me at a perfect time. I've been feeling the universe nudge me towards a bigger vision in my professional life, and this was exactly what I needed to help give me a little more courage to consider taking the next step... Mary Anne's expansion of her famous poem on courage is an excellent blueprint for navigating change with bravery and success. Step by step, this will lead you to find your life's greatest potential. Her wisdom, along with advice from some of her greatest influences, creates a guide that normalizes the challenges of practicing courage, gives permission to make mistakes and, most importantly, teaches you how to never give up on becoming your best self. This is the book that you will read, and share with others, again and again."

—Grady Brown, sports coach in Little Rock, AR

"Mary Anne's *Courage Doesn't Always Roar* is both career-changing and life-altering. It helps you have a deeper understating of courage—it isn't just the loudest, biggest, or the first. Courage whispers and roars. It moves fast and knows when to slow down and be methodical. It pushes forward and knows when to turn back. Courage doesn't always roar… but it is indeed intentional. Mary Anne's daily inspirations will have you living, or leading, a more intentionally courageous life."

—Robbie Hanson, operations executive and culture consultant, Portland, OR

"*Courage Doesn't Always Roar* is not a book to be read from front to back and certainly not in one sitting. Each essay asks us to reflect, to question the way we handle and incorporate life's twists and turns. Surprisingly, many of these essays can be applied to business—decision-making, finding clarity, handling obstacles, evaluating risk. Radmacher has a genius for honing in on the deceptively simple things that lead to consequential results. She clears away the over-complications and disorder of daily life and gently nudges us to examine what we do and why we do it. This collection will help you to see differently, to examine alternatives, and hopefully lead you to raise new questions that challenge the way you courageously navigate this world."

—Barbara Grassey, author and small business marketing strategist

"Courage, of course, comes from the French word meaning 'heart'—and this little book, which is titled from and expounds upon the author's well-known quotation that courage can simply be the resolve to try again tomorrow—is a wonderful compendium of ideas for how exactly to do that. As its subtitle suggests, author Mary Anne Radmacher takes a wide view of what courage can be and why this quality is so important to cultivate now. Set up to provide daily morsels for inspiration, each of the book's 189 short essays ends with a reflection question to deepen your understanding of that day's focus. Like all of the author's books, *Courage Doesn't Always Roar* is a work of heart—a thoughtful guide that will not only deepen your sense of the possibilities for demonstrating courage in your life, but also deepen your experience of life itself."

—Maggie Oman Shannon, author of *Prayers for Healing*,
  Crafting Calm, and *Have Hope*

COURAGE doesn't always ROAR

Other Works by Mary Anne Radmacher

Lean Forward Into Your Life

Simply an Inspired Life

Live Boldly

Live with Intention

May Your Walls Know Joy

Promises to Myself

Honey in Your Heart

Us!

She (published with Viva Editions)

Life Begins When You Do (published with Sourcebooks)

Live Your Best Story (part of the iDecide365 series)

COURAGE doesn't always ROAR

And sometimes it does.

Redefining courage
with daily inspirations

MARY ANNE RADMACHER

Conari Press
CORAL GABLES

For permission requests, please contact the publisher at:
Mango Publishing Group
2850 S Douglas Road, 4th Floor
Coral Gables, FL 33134 USA
info@mango.bz

For special orders, quantity sales, course adoptions and corporate sales, please email the publisher at sales@mango.bz. For trade and wholesale sales, please contact Ingram Publisher Services at customer.service@ingramcontent.com or +1.800.509.4887.

Courage Doesn't Always Roar: And Sometimes It Does. Redefining Courage with Daily Inspirations

Library of Congress Cataloging-in-Publication number: 2022931239
ISBN: (print) 978-1-64250-905-2, (ebook) 978-1-64250-906-9
BISAC category code PHI010000, PHILOSOPHY / Movements / Humanism

Printed in the United States of America

For Kathleen, who as a friend, inspires courage and provides kindnesses with every turning day, and who as a parent, modestly serves as a role model for those who want to raise their young humans to know a full range of autonomy and courage.

Plus she makes the best lemon bars on the planet, and children know enough to think she is a faerie.

Table of Contents

*Courage isn't always consciously intentional.
Sometimes it quietly operates in the background, like a soundtrack that
leads a dance of natural and organized responses.*

*Courage doesn't always know where it's going.
Sometimes it's the quiet intention that whispers,
"Let's just start and see what we see."*

*Courage doesn't always understand the sense of an action.
Sometimes it simply knows that a change is essential.*

*Courage doesn't always wait for every detail.
Sometimes courage just chooses a door and walks right through it.*

Courage cannot know the outcome from a single action.
It can quietly assure that kindness is never a poor choice.

Courage manages to speak up for itself and others,
even when the voice is barely a whisper and even when
it has to repeat itself.

Courage doesn't always get it right, not even the third time.
Courage is the capacity to bring it fresh to the field the tenth time
knowing it was only a matter of time.

Courage is not always in motion.
Sometimes it is the strength to pause, to stop, or to walk away.

"It is not the critic who counts; not the man who points out how the strong man stumbles, or where the doer of deeds could have done them better. The credit belongs to the man who is actually in the arena, whose face is marred by dust and sweat and blood; who strives valiantly; who errs, who comes short again and again, because there is no effort without error and shortcoming, but who does actually strive to do the deeds; who knows great enthusiasms, the great devotions; who spends himself in a worthy cause; who at the best, knows in the end the triumph of high achievement, and who at the worst, if he fails, at least fails while daring greatly, so that his place shall never be with those cold and timid souls who neither know victory nor defeat."

—Theodore Roosevelt,
April, 1910, from a speech at the Sorbonne

Foreword

by Candace Doby

"You've been bringing me inspiration every day in a rather indirect way."

This was the first line of the first email I drafted to Mary Anne Radmacher on August 18, 2012, to request an interview. I was a budding student of courage, eager to gather and dissect as much information about this virtue as my brain would allow. For months, I had been collecting books, magnets, and mugs of Mary Anne's words and adopting many of her aphorisms as personal affirmations. Eventually, everything I had learned from her at a distance compelled me to seek her out for a personal interview. It seemed like a grand idea; but almost as soon as the thought developed, a looming risk of rejection overwhelmed my initial excitement and urged me to abandon the plan in the name of self-protection.

Fears of failure, judgment, rejection, and humiliation often appear when we are called to discover, create, and elevate; they threaten to keep us stationary. But how are we to step into the fullness of our potential and gain greater access to ourselves if we are unwilling or unable to summon personal courage to face those threats and dance with uncertainty and possibility? This is an underlying question Mary

Anne's wrk invites readers to consider, and it's one I needed to ponder for myself on that day in August.

Mary Anne's unique and colorful contribution to the conversation on courage comes from her exploration of it as a foundational quality that both whispers to us and roars within us as we rally toward both everyday goals and long-term dreams. Courage can be the quiet voice that encourages us, as she famously posited, to try again tomorrow: to take another look, to speak up, or to send the email. It can also be the reverberating rumble that pushes us to change in support of growth—to start a new path and to begin again.

Through quotes, stories, questions, and images, Mary Anne remarkably helps us understand that there is no hierarchy to courage—that the power of courage cannot be either minimized or exaggerated based upon the immensity of the act for which it is needed. Courage is rather a steady and potent force that everyone has the capacity to call upon and to employ to help them take on risks related to *any* of the goals or pursuits they deem worthwhile.

On August 18, I had a goal: to connect with Mary Anne personally, not only to tell her how much she inspired me, but also to create an opportunity to learn from her directly. Emailing Mary Anne to request an interview felt both bold and terrifying. The risk of rejection was palpable…but so was the power of possibility. And it was because of that possibility that I decided to press send.

Mary Anne responded within one hour, cordially agreeing to the interview.

She has taught me, both through that particular experience and in a decade of friendship and mentorship as well, that courage never guarantees success, but it will always open the door to possibility. And she's also showed that possibility is not confined to grandiose acts. The depth of courage's power can be witnessed and wielded every single day. These are the same lessons she delightfully teaches readers in the following pages.

Indeed, courage doesn't always roar. But it *does* always deliver opportunities to recognize its power (and yours, too).

Candace Doby

Speaker and Courage Coach, The Can-Do Company

Author of *A Cool Girl's Guide to Courage*

Host of *The Courage Hotline* Podcast

Preface

Courage deserves a wider brushstroke of understanding. Conversations about courage generally lean toward the frontline professions, like workers who went to work at grocery stores in the face of a pandemic, firefighters in the grip of heat who resist the very human urge to step away from flames and instead run toward them, mental health professionals responding to domestic violence, public safety officers and military personnel who never know if their "see you later" is the last they will ever offer. Courage is present in all these professions, certainly.

Courage shows up in so many ways in ordinary days; the leader who chooses ethics over profit, the student who stands up to her friends rather than embracing acceptance or popularity, the person challenged by pain who puts a foot to the floor or slips into a wheelchair and moves into another day. Yes, getting out of bed can take some amount of courage. And these can as well:

- Speaking up.
- Judiciously remaining silent.
- Taking the time to thoroughly think through options at the risk of being accused of being slow or not committed enough.
- Having the capacity to listen hard rather than rushing to offer advice.

- Daring to dream.
- Attempting the untried.
- Leading into innovation.
- Facing unexpected events.
- Embracing change.
- Being vulnerable.
- Adopting unfamiliar practices in the search for fresh outcomes.

I could fill a book just with descriptions of circumstances that require a fresh consideration of courage.

I wrote a piece for a friend, a young mother, that ultimately became the poem.

Courage doesn't always roar.
Sometimes courage is the quiet voice at the end of the day saying,
"I will try again tomorrow."

Anyone who has ever faced a task so large that it felt beyond their capacity will understand this origin story. More than most, first-time parents can be overwhelmed with the 24/7 care of an infant and the length of the commitment involved for parenting. Imagine who might say yes to a job description that began, "You will be required to work 24/7 for approximately two decades. You will do this with no supervision and no training. There are no earned vacation days, and there is no available replacement: you will conduct this work when you are well and when you are sick. You will show up for this job when you feel like it and when you do not. Oh, and let me add, you will not be compensated in any monetary way—ever. There is a fair percentage chance that your work will someday pay you dividends in gratitude, appreciation, and love. But those returns are hard to quantify and are not guaranteed. Do you want to apply for this job?"

Um. No. I considered applying for that job myself: becoming a mother. And I chose a path that did not include having a child. I am filled with utter dazzlement and amazement for those who choose parenting and do so with passion, dedication, and love. In fact, I am known to bow to a mother or a father in a grocery store—or in any public place—who deals with a tired child in a measured, compassionate way. And I myself have laid down on the floor with more than a few screaming children just to catch their eye and give a wearied parent a moment to catch their breath. But. 24/7? I cannot conceive of the courage which that requires: courage, every day.

When a longtime friend came to my office in tears, uncertain that she had what was required to be a "good parent," I listened as hard as I could. I wanted to contradict her immediately and tell her what an awesome human she was, but I suspected she needed more than that. So, I listened. Her tears slowed. She went away feeling some better than when she came in. In the quiet of my office, with my door closed, I penned what would ultimately become a poem that has traveled the world, become the engraved welcome to cancer wards, been etched in metal on arches over military complexes, and is featured on firehouse doors at many precinct firehouses annually on September 11. I was gobsmacked in the days after the terrorist attack on New York's Twin

Towers. The poem first appeared on a regional web site for firefighters. I learned that as the days passed, more fire houses throughout New York and New Jersey had created banners with the courage poem printed on them and hung them over the engine house doors. It's what greeted the firefighters on each shift when they finally returned from their arduous work at Ground Zero.

I've been told so many stories over the years that humble me and make me grateful for my work in the world as a poet and an author. I remember a story shared by a mid-level administrator; she noticed at the end of one particular week that one of her coworkers seemed to be kind of down and struggling. She kept a stash of little cards I'd made available with the courage piece printed on them. When her coworker was away, late in the day, she slipped it into the center of his clear desktop. She figured it would greet him Monday morning: a bit of encouragement. The following week, that man confessed to her that it did more than offer a bit of encouragement. (I could write that enCOURAGEment.) He had come back to the office late that Friday night to make taking over his job easier for his coworkers, whom he much admired. He planned to take his life that weekend, and he didn't want to leave unfinished projects for his work friends. What he found in the center of his desk felt to him like an invitation to stay on the planet. He phoned a suicide hotline from his desk that very evening and got the support and help he needed. She told me this story providing kudos to me for my words, saying I'd saved a man's life. Correctly, I observed that it had required teamwork. I wrote that poem to lift up a friend. She shared it for the same reason.

I reached out to that longtime friend, Margo Lemons Dueber, who was caring for her grandchild at the time. I asked her if she had time to reflect back on that challenged day as a young mother. I asked her if she was willing to share her view of how it has traveled the globe over the years. This is what she had to share.

I am the friend who came to Mary Anne in tears, when I was so defeated and unsure of where to turn next. In my mind, I was failing miserably and quite possibly dooming my child to a life of misery. I remember the feeling that I couldn't do it anymore because I had no answers. Parenting is the most difficult job I've ever tackled.

*We all know that "Tomorrow is another day." But the **courage** words help us all to remember to listen to that quiet voice at the end of the day and to be at peace knowing we have another chance to make a difference. We all know how the years seem to fly and we look back in amazement at where we were and how far we've come. Mary Anne wrote those words so many years ago to uplift me. Over the years they have steadfastly done just that. To this day, I rely on them and keep them tucked away in my heart.*

The child who was my reason for complete despair recently sat beside me as we watched her beautiful daughter glide and

dance across the stage. And that child recently told me she
was glad I'm her Mom.

So, read with a focused and open mind these words of
courage. *And always, always listen to that quiet voice at*
the end of the day and be at peace.

If this poem calls to you and you have picked up this book, I hope you will enjoy the many unconventional ways I treat the quality of and capacity for courage. You won't necessarily read the word courage in each essay; just like courage itself, it shows up in quiet ways. And further, I hope that we can become teammates in lifting others up by using these twenty-two words to uplift them and give hope and en**courage**ment to others.

With a great amount of love and appreciation,
Mary Anne Em Radmacher

Courage isn't always consciously intentional.

Sometimes it quietly operates in the background, like a soundtrack that leads a dance of natural and organic responses.

Being alive is a fierce responsibility.

Breathing: it's a privilege lost to many. Being alive is indeed a fierce responsibility. It can become a dull habit to defer dreams and aspirations to an imaginary someday. Someday is imaginary because it is promised to no one.

Perhaps you cannot realize the fullness of all your deeply held aspirations in the present moment, but can you start? Can you take small steps toward the bigger thing?

A friend harbored a decades-long dream to live as an expatriate somewhere in Europe. Year after year, on her list for the coming months, she wrote these words: "Move to Europe." But once she went through the "Remember and Do What Matters" program, she recognized that deferring her dream was no longer an option. She gave herself permission to begin to act on this long-held yearning. She began cobbling together a plan. She then acted on the plan with specificity, one thing at a time. Each step had obstacles and resistance which she faced and moved beyond.

Now? She's writing about the expat life and the view out the window of her dwelling in a lovely fishing village in The Algarve of Portugal. That view is the vision she held for herself over years. Now it's her everyday view.

When you assume a fierce responsibility toward the desires for your own life, you can begin to make them happen.

Will you be fierce in your responsibility to your own aliveness?

2 | *A dream is an action. A dream is a longing, held deeply.*

Think of times you have said, "I dream of a day that I will _____ (go ahead, fill in the blank)." There are all kinds of signs, directives, and products inspiring you, all insisting that you dream big. Might I rather insist that you simply dare to dream? The magnitude matters less than the fortitude to allow your dream to rise up in priority.

Dare to dream that you:

- have the courage to imagine
- can live a life aligned with what matters most to you
- have the strength to embrace that you are worthy of something different or can embrace more of something you already have and love.
- The size of a dream will manage itself once you start exercising the muscle required to dream at all.

Of what might you dare to dream today?

3 | *Manifest a thing: Pair the best of your imagination and skills with your capacity for risk.*

Manifesting can either be creating something from nothing or it can be transforming more of something that already exists into something more apparent.

There is much talk of manifesting the desires and longings of the heart. There are numerous belief structures about this process. I return to the time-honored observations of Marcus Aurelius and the Stoic philosophers who inspired him:

- What we focus on expands.
- We see what we expect to see.
- Our experience often follows along behind our thoughts.

Once a clerk complained out loud in my general direction about spam calls and about the bags—complained and again complained. She declared what I had already observed: that she was having a terrible day. She asked if I would give her permission to go home and start over. I answered, even while recognizing her request could've been rhetorical, that she didn't need to go home to start over. Every second of every day provides the opportunity to start over, right where we already are. I asked if she was ready, and she stared at me. I snapped my fingers and said "Poof! Fresh start. Isn't it great that they are available on demand?" She was speechless. I took my purchase and said over my shoulder, "Enjoy the fresh start on your brand-new day." I suspect that a part of her enjoys complaining and didn't really want a fresh start. It requires a level of personal knowing to make that kind of a shift in thought and perspective.

Do you want to do what you've always done and get what you always get, or would you like to manifest something new today? What?

4 | *Do I really have time for this?*

It lives in my memory that an adult once responded to my defensive statement, "I didn't have time to do it," with, "You make time for what matters." It stung in the moment, yet in the decades that were to follow, the truth of it has become clear.

With more maturity and guidance behind me, the authentic explanation would have been some form of saying that I did not prioritize the project by the way that I managed my time. In this, there is the difference between an explanation toward understanding and an excuse to avoid responsibility.

Asking if you really have time for something can be elaborated to, "Does this align with what matters most to me?" And if it does, "Will I be able to commit to it in the context of my other promises and priorities?" A former publisher and editor, Paula Rudberg Lowe, made this observation: *"We choose what we do with our time. Being busy or saying we 'don't have enough time' are often excuses, which means other things (or people) are not a priority."*

Not everything that matters must be done immediately. But sometimes a thing has such an element of press that it bumps other promises as it makes its way to the very top of your priority list. Being clear on what is most important allows wise investment of your available moments, investment absent any excuses.

What will you invest your time in today?

5 | *Write intentions with divine ink. Craft plans in pencil.*

Divine Ink is your capacity to synthesize your instinct with your experiences and mix in some trust, a modest amount of optimism, and a substantial amount of resolve.

"It did not go as intended." It's easy to confuse an intention with a plan or an expectation. As I've embraced understanding of what it is to live an intentional life, I recognize many attributes and aspects. Writing intentions in divine ink represents a flow, a flexibility, a remarkable capacity to pivot.

To "turn on a dime" is a phrase often applied to accommodating unexpected or unanticipated events. I like it better in the context of a choreographed dance. In dance terminology, it's called a "ball change": The dancers shift their weight from one foot to the other in order to execute a dramatic change in direction. Perhaps divine ink choreographs, or even makes possible, a series of holy ball change moves.

Writing with divine ink allows one to remember and do what matters—to find ease and forward momentum of your own making in a circumstance that is undeniably frustrating or even unfair.

In that remembering, one can craft a plan—in pencil, a pencil with a stout and generous eraser. Plans of any sort are speculative regardless of the method for writing them. They start a process in a generally correct direction. The more you head in the general direction of your intention, the more both the greater clarity will emerge and you'll need that eraser to adjust your plan a little less often.

How can you make marks on the calendar of your days with your unique divine ink?

6 | ## Where is my pride of craft in relationship to this?

Your craft might be what you did before you retired. Or it could be what you primarily focus on in your employment. It might be the thing that engages your passion and attention as a hobby. Regardless of where it fits in your life, your particular craft is an important part of how you show up in the world.

Have I honored all I know about my craft in my current situation? How? There's a substantial difference between objective evaluation of a project and (chronic self-destructive) criticism.

Pride of craft is not to be conflated with perfectionism. Giving one's best to an endeavor doesn't imply it's perfect. It does mean that at this time, you have manifested the skills of your craft at their highest level to date. A lot of pride can be taken in that.

There are times when pride of and in the craft rises up from the simple act of starting or working toward completion. Even our craft likes our attention. There's pride in remembering we are capable of doing a particular thing. A gap in your confidence can inhibit your ability to wholeheartedly commit your creativity and attention to a thing. Call upon the wonder of your child-self, who had the pluck to make stuff and be inventive until it may have been schooled out of them.

How have you given thought to or participated in your own craft recently?

7 *Remember and do what matters.*

In order to remember and do what matters, you must first have clarity on the things that matter most to you.

When you have a clear measure (criteria and/or metrics) for what is essential, decisions come more easily. When everything feels urgent or necessary, choosing what to do first becomes more difficult.

Once you know what matters most to you, it is helpful to create a system unique to your way of being in the world that consistently reminds you of what your primary priorities actually are.

Do you know what matters most to you?

How do you remember what matters most at an inflection point? I use physical icons and images to help me remember. Pat Wiederspan Jones, instructor and artist, has chosen a Swiss cross as her iconic reminder. She explains why in this way: *"My balanced cross reminds me of my relationships—to self, to others, to place, and to time. Remember and Do What Matters is a focal point, along with this icon, and remains a strong influence."*

What will you choose as a visual reminder of what matters most to you?

8 | *Positive, proactive planning supports your intentions and respects the priorities of others.*

Planning is a wonderful exercise in allowing experience, expertise, math, and imagination to meet up and have a cuppa something together. Positive planning asks, "What if something goes right?" Proactive planning asks, "What's the next path if something drops in or something drops out?"

Kirstin Bolander Rich recognizes an application in this: *"My prefrontal cortex and I regularly struggle with planning and upfront thinking. Thanks to the way it is framed here, my paradigm around this is shifting. Planning (especially weekly) as an anticipated meet-up instead of dreaded drudgery! 'I will try again tomorrow.'"*

You've probably read or heard the phrase, "Poor planning on your part does not constitute an emergency on my part." A plan clarifies your intentions for a thing. The process of planning, creating an anticipatory, flexible structure, is a sign of respect both for yourself and for anyone else impacted by what you have in mind. Planning is not a signal for control. Rather it is a satellite beaming to the unexpected that you have both clarity of event and a readiness to pivot.

How can you plan this day using a flexible metric?

9 | *You see your world through the windows of your intentions.*

It's a familiar action: looking outside or into another space through a window. It's not always a panoramic view, but it's certainly more informative than staring at a wall. Your intentions inform any view. If a desire to serve is a core intention, a natural disaster becomes an opportunity to act upon your commitment. If your intention is to create or make a certain type of thing, a stormy day when you're confined at home by the elements becomes a chance to devote time to that specific endeavor. Being connected to the intentions you hold puts all your experiences in the context of living aligned to your promises and intentions, especially the ones you have made to yourself.

How are you looking at your immediate world?

10 | *One intention can generate myriad results.*

I am the daughter of a maker who worked in a production manufacturing plant most of his life. He modeled for me that one thing can do many things. I earned my way in the world and provided a good livelihood for dozens of people for over thirty-five years. I built my business continually learning ways that one thing can serve many needs. When the needs of your own core, your circle, and your community are served in a single action, *that* is profound alignment. This principle deserves study in order to replicate the synergy of it as often and in as many circumstances as possible.

How can you tell when the needs of many entities are being served by a single action?

11 | *Intentions work within even when they are not fully developed or named.*

An intention is synthesized from many things—longing, wish, capacity, imagination, calling, giftedness, compassion, and belief systems, to name only a few. Intention is the resulting long-burning fire rising from a cosmically well-laid structure. Your own sense of personal agency is the match, struck against self-knowing, to light the fire that is your intention. Although intention may be unconscious, it is not accidental. The consequences of an intention may create accidental or "unintended" outcomes, but the intention itself is not an accident. The more aware of and connected to your intentions you are, the more your daily choices will align with them.

How do you align your intentions to your choices?

12 | *Like a firework, a single action has ever outward consequences.*

The concept of ever outward consequences is a neutral one. The outward expansion of a consequence works equally on a negative intent as it does on a positive intent. It implies the consequence grows larger the further outward it expands. What would it look like if you drew out consequences of a single action, as you envision them occurring? As I contemplate my own development of a consequence map, I recognize the core of an intention is at the center of the "firework." It is ultimately followed by an unshaped imagined plan, which then initiates/shapes/forms into some kind of an action.

Picture a line of dominoes. *You* only initiate movement on one, and yet… "A single action has ever outward consequences." They all fall forward, or outward, or sideways, one by one.

There are many roads that lead out from this single concept. Some have legal considerations. Others draw toward moral responsibility. There is the whole "end justifies the means" consideration. In simplifying, perhaps oversimplifying, it all returns to initial intent and the will and agency tied to that intention.

Rather than attempting to follow all those different roads on this day, I simply embrace the courage to ask myself the question, "What is the core of my intention in choosing to take this specific action?"

What benefit would drawing a consequence map of a particular intention provide?

13 | *We tell the tale of our lives by the stories we repeat in our days.*

Marcus Aurelius, Stoic philosopher and one of the last good Roman emperors, wrote that the body goes where the mind goes. People have intuitively understood for centuries that the body believes what the mind tells it. Modern neurological research supports the understanding that this process is so much more than the power of suggestion. In fact, research is finding that every time you retell the story of a positive event, the body responds by generating endorphins and other hormones, particularly that feel-good hormone, oxytocin. Conversely, when relating a story of harm, danger, loss, or disappointment, the body registers many of the same traumatic impacts as when the event was first experienced. Expressed a different way, the body relives the actual experience of whatever story you are repeating, whether it is uplifting and inspirational or traumatic and negative. This is a simplification of a complex physiological and psychological function.

Consider that we have two sets of story blocks. The blocks that promote energy and growth are perfectly balanced. They stack neatly and well. The stories that steal energy produce discomfort and are structurally out of alignment. They create a stack that is wobbly and unstable. Courage makes changing the stories you tell more possible.

What are the stories you can call to mind that make up your stacks?

14 | *Whether it is hidden, lost, or regularly employed, everyone operates using their own chosen variety of compass.*

Dwight Eisenhower popularized the idea of a quadrant system of prioritizing tasks into four categories ranging in scope from *do immediately* all the way to *never do*! The quadrant as a metric is employed in things from human anatomy (heart, abdominal cavity) to urban planning to the time-honored compass referencing north, south, east and west. The compass remains useful even in modern times, even with broad access to GPS guides (global positioning systems).

The metaphorical compass is equally useful in navigating life direction. Over the centuries, the directions have taken on symbolism rich in metaphor and meaning. In feng shui, north is represented by the rat, signifying the qualities of adaptability and wit; the east is represented by the rabbit, with the qualities of trust and love; the horse gallops in to represent the south with strength and adventure; and the rooster crows from the west with confidence and persistence. In some indigenous cultures, there are diverse and abundant explanations for the four directions, which are held as sacred. The Lakota consider north the direction of wisdom and thought; east is where Spirit dwells, represented as redemption; beginnings and purity inhabit the south; and the west is the place for conclusion and fullness. These are a just a few examples among numbers of others.

If you created your own attributions on your own personal compass, what would they be?

15 | *Clarity has the nerve to decline all of the nonessentials in the course of a day.*

When I do a little bit of everything, I end up feeling at the end of the day that I've done nothing. Why? Because nothing is done, completed, *finished*! Sure, there's been progress on a lot of things and perhaps progress on many things that qualify as essential. Yet they are not essential in the context of the one thing that really needs to be completed in that day. Picture one of those trays of various flavored truffles. Somebody has taken a tiny bite out of every single truffle. Yet the tray remains full. With clarity it is understood that tasks declined as nonessential in one moment will show up as an essential task at another time, "at a time that is not now."

What might the day yield if the intentionally directed effort was focused on the one thing that matters most?

16 | *Does this align with what I say matters most to me?*

Opportunities.

Offers.

Requests.

Needs.

Actions.

Occasions.

Events.

Chances.

Demands.

Requirements.

Advancements.

Obligations.

Wishes.

Each day is filled to the brim with calls to action and appeals for money, for time, for attention. Feels like everyone and everything wants a little piece of you. That very phrase, "You wanna piece o' me?" popularized in movies from *Toy Story* to the comedy *Seinfeld*, is intrinsically confrontational. It implies the question, "Really? This is going to be a fight?" as well as the assessment, "Let's go ahead and fight." Swimming in the overly full waters of so many demands and choices can feel like a struggle, an outright fight for your attention. Time is finite, and moments of indecision cannot be called back nor redeemed. What to choose? Simply because a person is qualified or capable of a thing does not mean it is theirs to do.

Is there something you want to let go of? What is it?

17 | *Your no becomes someone else's yes.*

The panorama of a person's history provides information regarding what matters most. Clearly identifying the general qualities as well as the specific manifestations of what truly matters allows someone to align their choices with that; to clarify, to make a solid decision based upon what matters most to them. Succumbing to whatever request comes knocking first or the one request that beats on the door of your attention most diligently or loudly puts your time, resources, and energies all at the whim of others. Aligning your choices with what matters most to you requires first that you have a degree of clarity regarding what those things are. Without that intentional grasp, a day can feel splintered or like a fractured pottery bowl. Even if the pottery bowl is not broken to shards, the fracture takes away its capacity to act as what it is intended to be, a safe vessel or container for nourishment. Regret can follow closely behind such fractured attention, questioning every determination. Knowing your core values with specificity calibrates every choice you make with measured confidence. Remembering what aligns with what you say matters most to you requires first knowing what matters most! That alignment openheartedly invites ease in decisions and actions, purposely implemented without remorse.

Lynda Allen advocates for this principle in this way: *"Learning the lesson that your no is someone else's yes has been invaluable to me. It applies to jobs, relationships, tasks, everything! If something is not mine to do and I do it anyway, then I have taken that opportunity away from someone else."*

Additionally, Jean Robin Martell remarks: *"I've always been an 'I should' person. That never gets me anywhere except on a short path to guilt. Honoring my own priorities and promises helps me tend to the important things and see the possibilities presented to me. I participated in Em's course about determining and doing what matters most two times. Very helpful! I know that for me, even though what matters most doesn't change much, my prioritization of them can vary. I will think about and write about this more today while considering the possibilities presenting themselves."*

How, in a culture of FOMO (fear of missing out) and chronic *yes!*, do you have the gumption to offer an unapologetic *no*?

Connect to the lasting impact of what you say and how you say it.

Words cannot be unspoken nor taken back. Children try it all the time with, "Take that back!" In the real world of communication, unlike in games, there are no backsies. I return to the well of Maya Angelou's truth poured in this way, "When someone shows you who they are, believe them the first time."

Your intentions are mirrored in your words. Politicians often say what they actually intend and then have to clean up a PR mess with, "I misspoke. What I meant to say was…" Nonpolitical entities also speak their real thoughts first and then try to fix the consequences after the fact. Sociopaths deal with this by gaslighting. They blame others for the truth of what they've uttered by claiming they never said it or blaming the listener for misconstruing their intent.

There's nuance to language. The literal meaning often gives way to a more subtle message. Choose wisely. Words matter. Words last.

How will you focus to connect the impact and import of what you say and how you say it?

19 For the widest perspective, meet the unexpected with the full power of your intentions.

To employ the full power of your intentions, you must first be clear on what they are. Your intentions act as your inner compass, both setting and directing the many roads of your life.

Do you feel unsure of or disconnected from your intentions? Look at how you choose to spend your time. When the activities that you spend your time on produce joy, deep satisfaction, or great outcomes, you'll be able to follow those threads to the intentions you hold at your core.

How do you stay connected to the widest perspective of your intentions?

20 Plant the seeds of your intentions in the soil of your days.

It's easy to allow your time to unravel without vision or purpose. Ask anybody who has sat down with a media platform for a minute or two and then been shocked to discover they had spent two hours in the spot. A level of determination is necessary to consciously construct your time investment plan. Author Annie Dillard, in her book *The Writing Life*, has popularized this notion in this way, "How we spend our days is, of course, how we spend our lives."

How will you tenaciously plant the seeds of your intentions in the soil of your life?

21 | *If this were my last day on the planet, would this matter?*

Kim Jayhan Pique had occasion to ask herself that question on many days as she struggled with a life-threatening illness.

In most instances, this is a whimsical inquiry best utilized for dismissing small annoyances or moderate regrets. Yet it certainly has a place in consideration of large undertakings.

You may have one or two or more (eh hem) projects or tasks that you agreed to out of a sense of obligation. Maybe you agreed for some other reason that is actually out of alignment with what matters most to you.

Applied to a big thing, this question may provide the context for reconfiguring how you will approach any task or project. Keep in mind there *are* things, like dust on your baseboard or a sink full of dirty dishes, that wouldn't matter a bit if it were your last day. On ordinary days, those kinds of things *do* go a long way toward improving your quotidian practices and your general environment. On other days, it's wise to leave the dishes in the sink and go dancing.

What matters to you today?

Courage doesn't always know where it's going.

Sometimes it's the quiet intention that whispers, "Let's just start and see what we see."

Can I move forward without knowing exactly where I am going?

Proximal direction is an anatomical, medical term that has been co-opted into the world of planning and goal setting.

At a practical level, it means that if you are in Iowa and you need to rendezvous with a friend near Nashville, you don't need to have the specific address in order to start driving. You can begin your journey, pointing yourself toward Nashville. Sometime, as you are heading in the proximal direction, you'll likely get more detailed information! There are those for whom courage is required to operate without a fixed plan.

Paula Rudberg Lowe elaborates, *"I prefer an end point using a map, or if at a meeting or event, I need an agenda. When making food, I need a recipe. When playing music, I need a score. There are a few things I can do without knowing where I am going: exploring a new site while vacationing, and walking on a new trail."*

Transferred to skills or in creating, you need not know every element of a craft, every nuance of a process, before beginning it. How do you start? By starting. You start by starting. Whisper to yourself, "Begin. Simply begin."

What is the general direction of your next deep desire? What can you do to point yourself in that proximal direction?

23 | *When you jump into your dreams, are your eyes open or closed?*

A few years before I started my greeting card company, I wrote a letter to my mentor of my longing to start an art company, even though I had no business training or funding. I expressed how scary it seemed. In the letter, I explained, "The jump is so frightening between where I am and where I want to be. Because of all I may become, I will close my eyes and leap."

My mentor made a copy of the letter, circled that phrase in red, and wrote in the margin, "If you base your company on writing like this, you'll have a long and enjoyable career." It is one of the most life-changing pieces of mail I've ever received.

Less than a year later, I leapt. My eyes were not open. Occasionally, I wonder if I would've even managed to start my own company if I had seen the challenges ahead in operating what became a formal corporation. A few years ago, I released an updated and revised version of that statement. If for no other reason than that it's helpful to see where to land your feet when jumping into a dream, it now says,

"I will *open* my eyes and leap."

In what ways can you embrace the determination to open your eyes and still take a leap?

A beginning follows some sort of ending.

Philosophers have long observed the intimate interconnectedness between beginnings and endings. It is the way of nature. We have allowed endings to become tangled with forms of regret, sadness, and even bitterness and resentment. Physicists note that there is no "away;" matter cannot cease to exist, matter can only transform. When it stops being what it was, it becomes something else.

Aside from the common misconception that oil comes from decayed dinosaurs, hence the phrase "fossil fuel," it is formed over billions of years from biomass, primarily marine organisms. Transformation: Nature exists as profound faculty in the school of life, especially in the context of beginnings and endings.

We do not observe spring mourning the ultimate coming of summer. We see a natural giving way of one season to another. Winter does not stomp its metaphorical feet and insist on a twelve-month season all its own. Aren't the butterflies glad for that!

To deeply inculcate the truth of this relationship, that of beginnings and endings, allows for a continuum of grace and acceptance. It is the grace of knowing one thing ends and another begins, and acceptance of the natural grief at the loss or end of a thing, as well as embracing the anticipation of a beginning.

Can you be cognizant of the various ends and beginnings?

What pace do I want my momentum to have?

My momentum has variable speeds. It is inappropriate to expect oneself to keep the same pace in all applications.

When I am tidying my environment, my pace is zippy and quick, often enhanced by upbeat (and usually loud) music. I look every bit like Mary Poppins, twirling about and multitasking like a master.

When I am working on a poem, the editing process is thoughtful and purposeful. I read it out loud, slowly. I count the line cadence. I listen for the places where a phrase needs more structure or perhaps greater spaciousness. If I organized my environment with that poetry pace, it would probably take a full week to finish!

Here are words of caution. Do not let your momentum be defined by marching in the "used to be" parade. Your pace must be understood in the context of this present time, not compared to what you were able to do last year or in another decade. Do not require your stride to be in sync with those walking around you. It takes fortitude in both literal and metaphorical instances to proceed alone. Sometimes you'll lead the parade, and sometimes you'll be last in line.

Can you identify the finest pace for your most desirable momentum in a project today?

If I pursue this to a natural, predictable conclusion, what would that be?

Looking first at the threads that lead to a predictable, natural conclusion is a great place to start building a plan. No complicated moving parts, no layers of various systems…just a simple, organic understanding of how a pursued outcome usually unfolds. It is then that one asks (and tentatively answers) the what-if questions. What if it rains? What if no one shows up? What if the delivery of the specific piece for inventory needed in stock is delayed?

Having a fundamental baseline plan does not guarantee a specific result. It does provide a springboard, essentially of alternative plans for other eventualities. Knowing that even the natural and the usual outcomes often meet detours on the way allows a plan to accommodate what would otherwise be unanticipated.

How might this be relevant to your day?

What you build is as important a consideration as where you build it.

Building evokes an image of a structure. It could be a structure going from the ground level up. like an iconic New York skyscraper; or perhaps an image more like Jimmy Carter with his carpenter belt on and hammer in hand, building for Habitat for Humanity.

I think in a circular way, so I envision building as concentric circles radiating ever outward. Throw a stone into still water and watch the resulting ever-widening impact. Circle upon circle, that single stone builds outward in ripples.

Having this kind of visual model to accompany a decision and strengthen it is a helpful tool.

What are you building today? And where is it you are building it?

28 | *Small is a good place to start.*

In a culture that celebrates grand gestures it takes a stout heart to wonder if a small launch/unveiling/pilot might work and then act on the wondering.

"Start small: Your first effort doesn't have to be a big production."

"Done is better than perfect."

I have a process habit of first creating a convoluted, complicated plan before I then peel down the layers to something that is simple and manageable. You might ask: Why use a fire hose when a garden hose will do? That's what I try and ask myself! That first plan sounds impressive by virtue of its complexity. However, measured by access and impact, it's not very spectacular.

Procrastination more easily shows up when someone says, "This is the list of *all* I've got to do before I can even start to think of starting." It is very true that some things must come first and early in a project or idea or event, but not everything. I often test before I fully implement. I think of all of the products I tested in my stores before considering releasing them at a wholesale level. They were imperfect—they were a beginning, they were each a great test. That small unveiling taught me many things that I couldn't have otherwise predicted. I saw firsthand if the products did not resonate with my customer niche. Ultimately, it made national product launches that much better. In some cases, I learned not to go to a larger distribution.

Will a small test work for one of your ideas?

29 | *Live as if this is all there is while being responsible to the promise of your future.*

What an opportunity I have to live among monarch butterflies. The metamorphosis I get to observe is awe-inspiring. I've watched a monarch as its chrysalis changes. I have witnessed the emergence. Like papers being unfolded from a precision origami project, the butterfly opens its wings fold by fold. Slowly they take their full shape. To the eye, it is a fully formed wing, yet the butterfly is not ready for flight. The butterfly must take the time to allow the waste material to disintegrate, and the wings must go from wet to dry. This can take hours. Just because the wings are unfurled does not mean the butterfly is ready to fly.

Right timing matters. It may look as if you are ready to fly, and yet only you know when the wings of your dream are dry enough for flight.

How do you discern when you are ready to launch?

30 | *Accepting and synthesizing various attributes leads to an integrated life.*

Considering the heart as the center of all strong feeling is an attitude held throughout the millennia. A strong feeling generates a measurable response in the heart area, a pounding, a flutter. The increase in blood flow is felt in the chest cavity. It's natural to believe it originates there. However, it begins in the brain and belly; in the heart and head, the mind, body, and spirit. People often reference them as if they are completely separate things. In an aligned life, they are cohesive, inseparable companions.

When a decision is made, it occurs as a result of synthesizing information, experience, and instinct (i.e., cogitating). What is often explained as a heart-based decision is really a brain and/or belly-based decision that empathetically and compassionately includes all the feels. What feels like a completely distinct physical decision actually has a lot to do with the primitive part of our brain called the amygdala. A lot of the "feelings" we experience originate in the brain. Just as humans do not live in isolation, neither does the heart. There is every reason for emotional and cognitive processes to live and navigate together for a life lived in harmony.

Have you noticed if you tend to view your heart-based decisions as a separate function from the way your brain operates?

31 | *It's a mountain full of unknowable mysteries, so start climbing.*

Published in 1957 in *Readers Digest*, this is attributed to Allen Saunders: "Life is what happens to us while we are making other plans."

We plan. We strategize. We establish goals.

We create metrics to measure the success of all of those things, and then as they say, "Life spills in." More accurately, life unfolds. And our plans are what spills in, or out! I favor planning in the same way that I favor using a map and my GPS. A GPS still faces roadblocks and calculated detours, just like a plan.

We take comfort in believing we have a path into our future, but the future is a mountain full of unknowable mysteries. In fact, it's a hard truth that we do not know the measure of our own future. So? Start climbing. Your next step is the only one you can be certain of.

Is there a step you can identify and take today?

What if there were no perceived negative consequences?

When contemplating a new venture or decision, it's natural to imagine all the things that might go wrong. It's a human way of engineering an event and preparing strategies for dealing with various potential mishaps, but one planning strategy that is often overlooked is preparing for potential *positive* outcomes. What if the answer to all the proposals is *yes*? How about if you actually win the bid on the house of your dreams? What would it feel like to imagine the outcome to the question, "What if something goes right?" instead of asking, "What if something goes wrong?"

Dr. Susan Paul Johnson contemplates this here: *"Hmmm…it occurs to me that sometimes I get more stuck in not starting because of all the things that could go right and wondering how can I keep it up. A question I ask myself is: What if we didn't judge outcomes? How about if we just let the consequences be what they are, and let them move us forward? After all, we only have control over what we put out there, not what happens with it."*

Will you find ways to wonder what will happen if something goes right?

Is there a physical place ideally suited to this activity?

As a journeyman mechanic also skilled in many other production crafts, my father often repeated, "Right tool, right job." In this context, I suppose he may have added, "right place."

There is one impulse in the school of just-get-it-done that insists that you make do with what you have. The concept of using what you have is a significant one. It supports resource management and stretches the imagination. An ideal physical space can be pivotal to the success of certain endeavors. I have steered clients toward creating their own ideal physical place suited toward their specific objectives: art room, jewelry bench, writing nook, or studio. Now, I always find a way to establish dedicated studio space. I've had my years of fitting in my creative space at the end of a kitchen table. No longer! Often, fueled by uncertainty or a lack of confidence, a creative will believe that their activities do not merit a space of their own. They do. Half the dining table, your lap, or a section of the kitchen counter will work for a stretch of time. However, if the endeavor is considered in the context of the ideal, you may benefit from remembering a reframe of my father's oft-repeated phrase, "Right effort, right place."

Can you claim or create a space that is appropriate for your vision or practice?

34 | *What is my first step toward understanding?*

A first step toward understanding is always an inquiry. There are two exceptions: when one chooses to observe and when one chooses to listen. So before a question arises, observe. Observe the parts you can see. So many misunderstandings occur because the viewer believes they are seeing the whole thing when in fact, their sight line only provides a partial view.

Listen. This is a partner to observation. Wholehearted listening often delivers understanding, or at least a deeper insight.

And then comes asking, making an inquiry. Asking questions based in a genuine desire for discovery and understanding can be a default first step. These are two elements in a three-part process.

How will you apply observing, listening, and asking?

35 | *Understanding things in the context of attributed color deepens understanding.*

Interdisciplinary education enriches student experiences. In the same way, applying seemingly unrelated metrics to a project or decision can expand the grasp and understanding of it. When I attribute colors or a single color to an actual project, it informs me at several levels. By project, I mean any project, not an art project. There are pending projects waiting on me. They are a muddy gray color, and I resist them. Attributing a color to one of them helps me understand that I must change my attitude toward it so I can approach it without a feeling of dread. Ascribing an actual color correlating to the nature of a thing helps me understand it more clearly. It informs me in a deeper way regarding how I actually feel about it. Everyone's color preferences are as individual as their task preferences. If you are puzzled as to why you continually defer a particular task or project, investigate it further by assigning a color to it. Perhaps looking at a color wheel would be a helpful resource. Color coding certain types of categories is a common office practice. Assigning colors to levels of priority for tasks is a long-standing method of planning. This color-assigning process takes that same technical practice into a deeper realm, the realm of acceptance and resistance.

What color is the next project in your immediate plan? Does applying the color impact how you think about it?

36 | I am not the same having seen the moon shine on the other side of the world.

I wrote that phrase on a hilltop in Wales while the sun was setting before me and the moon was rising behind me. There's a clear fearlessness involved when you choose to pack a small amount of familiar belongings and go somewhere completely unknown. The result of that courage has been one of the most rewarding actions of my life. From my first international trip decades ago when every dime I possessed was tucked against my belly in a very uncomfortable, plastic money belt, to my most recent international hop with a backpack and a journal...travel has trained me in claiming personal agency in a way that no home-based activity ever could. To travel as an explorer, not a tourist, trains the eye toward noticing and gives the soul the chance to encompass new ways of navigating life, regardless of location. Travel can recalibrate body, mind, and soul and the internal compass. Taking a journey lets one fall in love with this ridiculously suspended, fast-spinning orb called earth time and time again.

Can you dream of your next adventure and take a step toward it?

37 | *I cannot know how it will end. I am clear on how it will begin.*

We may not be in charge of all of the endings in our lives, but we can be exceptionally clear on most of the beginnings.

When I started my company in 1986, which was kicked off by a gallery show, I was clear on my intention. I wanted to provide affordable, original art that inspired people. That intention remained true throughout the decades of the body of work I created. The company I built, in the form that I created it, ended in a way that I would never have purposely chosen. Yet the clear intention that I formed at the beginning of my career has carried forward, and the work itself carries on as well in the hands of other visionaries.

Lynda Allen often reminds readers through her poetry and meditations that we can pause and choose how we will enter any moment and what we will bring to it.

There are accidental beginnings. Perhaps a chance meeting ends in romance. There are purposeful beginnings that are mapped out with a meticulously chosen route which eventually encounters detours. The clarity of a beginning lies first in the intention that is held; only then is it followed by focus, decision, or action.

Is there a space for a clear intention to kick off a clean beginning?

38 | *Have I set the right materials for a long-burning fire?*

Ask any well-trained scout! A specific process is required to build a long-burning fire. If you want impressive big flames for show, throw a bunch of stuff in a fire circle willy-nilly. With enough starter fluid, you'll get big flames. They will likely burn out quickly. Setting materials, however (which implies having first gathered the correct materials), and layering them in a specific structure supports a long-burning fire. It takes planning and specific actions. Other fires may flame up in advance of the fire you are building. But your fire will be burning long after others burn out. What may appear as fussy or annoyingly meticulous at the front end turns out to be an investment in long-term results.

The metaphor is evident. You and your endeavors are a long-burning fire. Be certain you have gathered the right materials around you to sustain your long-burning fire. The benefit of the extended light and warmth is worth the front-loaded effort.

What are the things you need for your long-burning fire?

39 | *Build a fire where it will deliver maximum benefit.*

I love this metaphor. I use it a lot. Building a fire is a natural model for an incredible variety of applications. A fire can accomplish great things, from the smallest embers to the most bodacious bonfire.

Ask a scout. Building an effective fire is a skill I was taught early on. Locating a fire appropriately is not only a safety concern, it optimizes the benefit of a well-built fire.

The fire triangle is an ideal model for decisions and actionable items of all sorts. The fire triangle is comprised of three things:

- **Fuel**—Kindling and sustainer, it must be appropriate to ignite and maintain the desired heat;
- **Air**—Your breath ignites the first flame—it needs oxygen to stay lit;
- **First Heat**—The starter, most often a match.

As to the fuel…a fire builder must start small. Using things such as shavings, twigs, and other small dry kindling give a sustainable fire the best beginning. If you've ever tried to start a fire with a big, heavy chunk of wood, you know that it rarely works. Start small, then add the big pieces once the flame catches and burns hot. (Flashing metaphor alert.)

Consider the physical model of the fire triangle. What makes up your fuel, air, and heat in the decisions you make today, and where will they produce the greatest benefit?

If you build this vision of yours as if it were a fire, where will it produce the greatest benefit?

40 | *If I achieved this, how would I feel?*

A process utilized in most business settings is this: Set a goal, identify the components necessary to achieve that goal, then get it done. How do you confirm success in this metric? The answer to that is usually a quantifiable answer. Success is measured by something like money earned or number of tickets sold, a specific objective acquired. This metric focuses only on the actual actions required to meet the goal, not the perspective that is necessary to successfully implement the steps on the way to completion of the goal. Traditional business measurements, even the commonly used decision tree processes, leave out this important question: "If I am successful in this, how do I imagine that I would feel?" Asked a different way, "What state of being or state of mind do I imagine experiencing if this particular thing is completely successful?"

Jeanette Richardson Herring uses this question a lot. She explains, *"When I wrote this question, I was considering creating something I hadn't done before. I often like to visualize or pre-visualize what having, being, or doing that would feel like and look like. If the feeling is joy, satisfaction, or peace, the knowing is that I helped, served, and/or learned in pursuit of following that path— then I'd know it's worth achieving. If it's worth achieving, it's worth doing with all my heart. From small to large projects, spiritual to tangible, it helps me to think about what the end result feels like."*

When I have a Big Thing to achieve, I also ask this question of myself. Once I identify how it might feel to achieve my aspiration, I go ahead and give myself a head start. I take steps to put myself in that state of being or state of mind in advance of actually achieving it. It places me in what author Carol Dweck calls a growth mindset. Connecting to how I imagine feeling when successful broadens my perspective and deepens my ease with pivots and changes in plans. Keeping my focus on how I will feel once the objective is completed enables me to handle obstacles more easily. I can learn and adjust in the midst of the inevitable unanticipated setbacks.

Do you have a Big Thing Kind of Dream? Say *why not?* and start imagining now how you would achieve it. Caren Albers says that the often provided advice of "fake it until you make it" sounds dishonest. She likes to think about it as "act as if." If someone's going publish a book, do what a person does who publishes a book. Research the steps and stages, and start walking as confidently as you can in that direction. By acting "as if," you experience the feelings of what it is like to achieve your goal all along the way, not just in the end. It can still feel scary, but you don't have to wait for something to happen to feel happy, proud, strong, and gratified. You're already doing it!

In what ways can you precipitate your success by imagining how it will feel to have already done it?

41 | *Decide when to decide.*

In her therapeutic practice, Brandie Sellers often asks, "Is this the best time to make a decision?" *Now* is not always the ideal answer. There are things that qualify the quality of a decision: input; considered reflection; evaluating available and potential resources; time; identifying impacts and likely outcomes. These are just some of many considerations that make up a good decision.

My answer about the best time for a decision for something that is not immediate or safety-threatening is *choosing* a time. Select a hard stop and put it on the calendar if it is days away, or set a digital reminder if the time for the decision is hours away. Deferring to "some other time" without specificity is how things never get decided. Chronic deferral without a date or time becomes burdensome, turning into rolling procrastination. A decision with a hard stop delivers the reputation of follow-through. That means when you say to someone,

"Let me think about it and I'll get back to you tomorrow by noon," that individual knows that you mean it.

More importantly, *you* know it, too. As Caren Albers knows, "That kind of accountability and following through for yourself provides the framework for living a contented life. Intentions stated and acted on create harmony. I agree some decisions are for now and some require more information and more careful study. But don't wait too long expecting to have all the answers figured out in an ironclad way. Decide and then decide again if you need to."

If you defer a decision, will you also add a specific date by which you will decide?

42 | *It's important to determine you have what is essential to accomplish what matters most.*

Critical materials supply: It's an industry term for certain availability of everything required to complete your vision, task, or product. The statement itself includes the word critical. In a home-based application, assuring the materials supply for a recipe means checking your spice drawer and cupboard for all of the ingredients required. Only the person getting ready to implement the project knows if substitutions are acceptable. If substitutions are reasonable, you get to ask yourself what you already do have that can be used.

I was among the first of my industry peers to absorb the remarkably higher cost of using recycled paper. At that period of time, there was a limited supply of high recycled content paper stock. The restriction of supply produced an insecurity of availability. I had to purchase bulk quantities of large-size sheer parent stock to make certain I could fulfill my product orders in a consistent and dependable fashion. It took some professional grit, given the limited availability of materials, to declare on every printed product that it was made from recycled paper. These decades later, there are broad ranges of recycled content papers available and access is more of a guarantee. This underscores that a certain supply has its own arc of availability. What was once scarce could become readily and broadly available.

Evaluating the critical materials supply for a unique enterprise or endeavor is a matter of assessment. If a consistent, predictable outcome is necessary, then the securing of source really matters. If the elements required have a range of replacements (which in manufacturing is called an acceptable variable), then sourcing can be more casual. This type of advance planning isn't always relevant; however, when it is relevant, it becomes a top priority if predictable success of the outcome matters to you.

Ask yourself and clarify, "Are the sources for my critical materials secure?"

43 | *Natural offshoots and innovations can rise from seemingly unproductive efforts.*

What might come of this? Are there secondary considerations I might be overlooking? Are there even third outcomes, tertiary results? The endpoint is such a giant focus that often the potential offshoots are overlooked or incorrectly categorized as failures. It requires a certain kind of tenacity to find a useful place for something.

Perhaps you know that the ubiquitous Post-it note is the result of a failed effort of a scientist at 3M named Spencer Silver. In 1968, he was working toward a formula for a strong adhesive that could work in all forms of transportation applications. What he got was a new material light enough to be easily removed and repeatedly applied. At first (pardon the pun) its ultimate application was not obvious. Post-it notes were first introduced to the marketplace in 1980. In a personal twist on that release, I was part of the test market. In cooperation with 3M's marketing team, Post-its were given to attendees at a conference I presented. Every person there was skeptical of any practical use for this small, yellow stack of papers. However, once I repeatedly demonstrated their various applications and effectiveness, that resistance became unmitigated enthusiasm.

Attempting to imagine potential offshoots is speculative. Simply acknowledging that alternative uses may be generated is the way to begin. That an offshoot may be produced is only proven in the curious pursuit, the open-minded doing of the thing—a willingness to engage with a discovery. The process of a natural offshoot is a fantastic way to reframe the assessment of failure. The primary objective may have been to create *that*, and instead you generated *this*. Boom! Failure transforms into discovery and surprise. Determination is mandatory for this type of discovery. Poet Theodore Roethke summarizes neatly, "I learn by going where I have to go."

What journey of discovery can you generate from things that did not meet their original objective?

44 | *Dare to create.*

Myths over millennia involve the dynamic magnitude of the power to create. This ability is a hallmark of deities and goddesses. Across cultures, there are commonalities related to the power of making something from nothing in every creation story.

The power to create is intimately tied to many measurable benefits:
- Fearlessness
- Innovation
- Discovery
- Willingness to fail
- Healing
- Clarity
- Problem-solving

To create anything, to be a maker, is to manifest a quality of mythic proportion and to exercise a primordial urge.

The compulsion of every living thing is the impulse to create life, to create necessities that support life such as beauty, making marks, the bliss of crafting meaning. It is evidenced in the creative play of children that making for the pure pleasure involved in the action is reason enough.

To create is to lay a footprint that might not be washed away by the incoming tide for quite some time.

The courage to create is a muscle. How will you build it today?

Courage doesn't always understand the sense of an action.

Sometimes it simply knows that a change is essential.

Change of any sort requires courage.

There are people whose study is the nature of the phenomenon of change. It is a profession; an entire industry has risen out of the need to assist in managing change. Structurally speaking, some consider that there are three types of change:

- **Static:** A linear shift where only two conditions are measured—before and after.
- **Dynamic:** When changes are measured in a planned arc. Step-by-step, with necessary adjustments, this type of change is monitored, managed, and measured from beginning to end.
- **Chaotic Kinesis:** Essentially, chaos! Unpredictable, and it's hard to plan for a completely unexpected change. This type of change is best understood in the context of a tsunami, or more likely, an evacuation of your home due to a busted pipe and ensuing flooding. In quick order, decisions must be made, like what to grab, what essentials must be protected, and then where to go?

In each of these defined instances of change, success as a metric includes adaptability and resilience. There are those who actively and willingly admit that they do not like change. Furniture stays put. Plans remain fixed. Dependable habits are reinforced. Here's an undercurrent that is often overlooked, and it is a lesson that lives outside our doors every day. Change is a sure sign of life. Consider egg to caterpillar to chrysalis to butterfly. Consider the seed becoming a blossom. Look to the sapling that ultimately bears fruit. Winter changes to spring. These changes are organic and natural. Humans change; the decision to do something differently that is outside of habit or comfort requires nerve, as well as the momentum that is required to manifest that change.

What are the qualities required for you to manifest any kind of change?

46 | *Contingencies are a part of the game.*

Some people call preparing for an apparently contradictory possibility "hedging their bets." More people consider the concurrent preparation of a Plan A and a Plan B to be infinitely appropriate. Establishing a fully articulated contingency plan while completely embracing a primary plan is just good math—there is a substantial percentage likelihood that random, unanticipated events will thwart your articulated and polished Plan A.

So, if not this, then *that*. Two seemingly different routes can ultimately deliver you to your desired destination.

Do you have a Plan B? Can you call it Plan A 2.0?

47 | *Change occurs unbidden. Being in choice makes change welcome, by invitation.*

Change will elbow its way to the front of your line. You may as well invite it to the front of the line to stand with you. Cheryl Craigie affirms, *"This resonates with me. I'm a big believer in the power of conscious choice. So many things in life are out of our control, but we can choose how to respond. This takes practice, of course, but choosing how to respond gives you some agency."*

An individual can resist the winter season all they like, declare that they hate the cold, and even travel constantly to chase the sun. Regardless, winter comes, welcomed or unwelcome. Seasons change in their natural, objective cycle, and resistance serves no good in the attempt at changing that cycle. The best that one might do is accommodate the change instead of resisting it.

What would go differently if you welcomed change?

48 | *Follow the unpredictable path toward innovation.*

It's been said in myriad ways that if you do what you've always done, you'll get what you've always gotten. Having comfort in specific processes can be a real asset. And certain systems have a life cycle, and it's difficult to discern exactly when it's beneficial to create change. These kinds of shifts from comfort to transition require both commitment and fortitude. The beginning question is simple: Is an innovation necessary for this particular application or process?

There are small actions that can help turn toward larger shifts in your practice and path toward innovation. Some of these actions to build your innovation muscle are:

- a new route to a regular location
- a different grocery store altogether
- someone else's favorite recipe or a different version for a dish that you have been preparing the same way for years
- a fresh format for a regularly scheduled meeting

Questions that promote innovation are:

- Is this a habit or does it exist because of proven effectiveness?
- Is there someone else doing this differently in a way that may challenge my existing assumptions?
- What are some of the ideas that I have previously dismissed, and shall I reconsider them?

Some of the most lasting and best innovations I have facilitated have come from asking teams to generate absurd, wild suggestions. Following what first appears to be a ridiculous thread often leads to the innovation path.

What questions will lead you toward innovation?

49 | *Repetitive actions create a cosmic choreography.*

There is a cosmic choreography made up of patterns designed with repetitive actions. The trick, as is often the case, lies in noticing. What patterns can be seen?

Repetitive patterns exist in layers of our lives. The opportunity to learn from them and leverage them for our own benefit occurs when we choose to identify them. Without conscious awareness of the activities we do on a loop, they are simply unconscious redundancies. When we purpose to observe the things we habitually do, however, we have the power to do at least these two things:

- Transform the consistent harmful bits into things that serve our vision for ourselves more effectively
- Deepen the habits or other bits of these patterns that support the ways we want to navigate life

Caren Albers wrote in her book *The Happiness Junkie*, "This idea of repetitive actions (habits) was one of the final pieces in my healing journey." In *The Biology of Belief*, Bruce Lipton explains that our habits function in the unconscious, leaving the conscious mind to do other things. We don't realize habits are reactions to previous stimuli running automatically in the background of our minds. Unless/until we recognize this, they will continue to be automatic.

"First we make our habits, then our habits make us."
—Charles Noble

Noticing it makes you the intentional Dance Director of your cosmic choreography, not simply allowing reflexive habit to be in charge.

What are the patterns you notice in your actions today?

50 | *Roll out the red carpet on the kind of day that you want.*

Opening your inner world to the possibility of glory and bliss in your external life is like rolling out the red carpet on the kind of day that you want. Marcus Aurelius observed that the happiness of your life depends upon the quality of your thoughts. Philosophers have been echoing these truths, found in the document called *Meditations*, for over 2,000 years. Aurelius was dramatically influenced by the Stoics Heraclitus and Epictitus. Even so, it is the body of work from this Roman emperor and statesman, Marcus Aurelius, that has echoed through the centuries and sustained a dramatic presence.

We make up the nature of our red carpet, our invitation to the kind of day we want to experience, by the things we focus on and the people and information we allow to influence us. With irony, Leanore Curran comments, *"It's too easy to lay down a red carpet for others and forget to use it ourselves."* Fundamentally, it returns to our core intentions and how they show up on any particular day. Reflect on these two contrasting experiences—a day with news broadcasts in the background of all you do and a day with your favorite music playing as the soundtrack to your day. Contemplate the differences of those two constructs.

What red carpet invitation will you offer to this day?

51 | *Pursue equanimity, equity, equality; as well as justice, kindness, fairness, and access and inclusion.*

In community, I am both an inviter and invited—both or either. How do you offer the invitation and answer it? As Lynda Allen acknowledges, *"It feels like a big question. Maybe with small actions each day, noticing my biases, wondering about people I haven't wondered about before, being open to conversations, and open to noticing and changing my perspective. These are pursuits I can and want to act on."*

It is observed repeatedly that we are stronger together. Humanity inhabits a single planet. Finding ways to fit in without creating systems that inappropriately exclude is a challenge for the entire globe. Pursuit of a justice that is equitable is the calling of every conscious human.

How can you work toward these goals today?

| *What am I resisting?*

Resistance can provide clues that appear to point in opposite or contradictory directions.

Some resistance serves as a warning. It is a message that is experienced at a cellular level, sometimes almost at the level of a whisper. It can sound like, "This is not good for you, avoid this."

Another experience of resistance is not a warning but an invitation. It may sound like, "This is the other side of your comfort zone." The other side of this invitation contains unparalleled learning and growth.

To choose to explore that which you resist requires a specific resolve. On both accounts, warning or invitation, it's easier to ignore your own resistance and maintain a status quo. Recognizing or exploring your levels of aversion is a journey populated with change and reward. Noticing this and embracing what you learn from the view nets long-term benefits.

Will you pay attention to what you resist in the day? (What you resist holds messages for you.)

53 | *Asking for necessary help is a signal of strength, not weakness.*

Lay minister Beverly Kipp uses these questions: "Can it wait? Do I need help now? Ask."

First, ask yourself, "Can it wait?" If there is no discernible harm in a wait mode, then wait. If there is a potential downside on waiting to act, ask yourself, "Do I need help now?" If the answer is yes, then ask.

Asking for help is fraught with anxiety and resistance for some people. Think to the times that a beloved of yours asked for help. Were you happy to give it? Were you glad they asked? Turn that around for you! It applies both ways.

In a culture that elevates those who go it alone, who pull themselves up by their own bootstraps, there is powerful implicit messaging that if you are strong, you will do it all yourself. But those who know understand the grit and strength involved in asking for and receiving the help that is needed. (I digress, but have you ever thought about that phrase? I know what the metaphor's intention is, but it seems to me pulling yourself up by your bootstraps borders on an Olympic-level gymnastics activity!)

Watch for the impulse to resist asking for help. This one inquiry courageously:

- busts assumptions
- tamps down anxiety
- expands possibilities
- elevates experience
- lifts the mind out of loop/replay cycles

Go ahead and ask! It changes the trajectory of a difficulty.

How can you override the impulse to resist asking for help today?

54 | *What is my arc of influence?*

Here are two categorical answers that come immediately to mind: first, the known, and second, the unknown or rarely known. The mental model of the Butterfly Effect asserts that the smallest of changes can have impacts of significant magnitude. The slightest tip of a plane's wing ultimately changes the trajectory of its flight. Think back. In your own history you may find a thing that appeared inconsequential at that moment yet ended up becoming the pivot point of a measurable life shift. The thing about the arc of influence is that beyond what is able to be identified, choices have tones of consequence that hold their sound beyond an individual's capacity to hear. Unseen, unheard, your influence travels ever onward to countless others.

If you accept this premise, does it impact the manner in which you make choices today?

55 | *A surprise waits at an intersection.*

This is true, almost always. An intersection creates something that is unexpectedly other from the two distinct roads (ways, things, people, ideas) that cross paths. Will you live in the intersection

between the magical and mundane,

between potential and practical,

between you and me?

Infinite possibilities dwell in the place where things that matter intersect.

How can you spot an intersection of ideas?

56 | *Adapt the map.*

A phrase that Marci Moore, author of *Love Letters From Your Life*, often used was, "Adapt the map." By that she meant plan a route. When plans change or unexpected opportunities arise, adapt the map. Change the plan. Adapt. To adapt recognizes flexibility over rigidity. Adaptability provides both ease and acceptance. Adapting is an essential tool of the realist. It means knowing that not all things will go according to the original plan or intention. Once new information is made available, the route, the plan, the party (whatever it is) can incorporate the new bits and carry forward. It may mean changing the planned route in order to get to the destination. It could even mean changing the destination itself. This does not mean making a judgment against the original plan—it doesn't make it wrong. Circumstance dictated a change, and wisdom adapts and finds a way to carry on.

Weaver Maxine Rothman notes, "I especially like when *adapt* becomes *adept*."

How will you find a way to become adept at adapting?

57 | *Follow the divine whisper of possibility.*

My waking whisper is an echo of what was murmuring in my ear as I hoped for sleep just hours before, "The seeds of possibility are sown in the soil of challenge." Sown. Murmured. Whispered. And in these days, shouted, also. In the face of crisis, chaos, challenge, it can be hard to discern that which is divine. In the cacophony of unrest, in blaring uncertainty, the holy moment, the sanctuary that is spirit, is both difficult to see and hard to find. I begin to find it in the profound and undeniably consistent beauty of form. In the whole of the universe, we have the physical reminder of the remarkable order that exists within and alongside apparent chaos. All living things share at least a single commonality: They grow. Growth is a defining condition that separates living things from nonliving things. To take that a little further, nonliving things may not grow, but they do change. There's the core whisper I hear: Everything changes.

Yes, everything changes. Cheryl Craigie tells me, *"Having spent close to thirty years in corporate life, I'm intimately acquainted with the unfamiliar (change) and know how difficult and scary it can be for some. I agree with Kanter's Law, that 'Everything can look like failure in the middle.' I also embrace another idea, this one from James Clear, that says, 'Your favorite artist's first work was just as bad as yours. Keep going.' Learn to embrace the unfamiliar, learn to make course corrections as necessary, but get to the finish line.*

You'll learn so much along the way and develop the resilience needed for tackling future unfamiliars."

The egg to caterpillar to chrysalis to butterfly to humus: Even a succession of seemingly unchanging days are cycling toward a seasonal transition, they are illuminated by a changing moon, and the body's cells are engaged in a continual and unseen march toward change.

Possibility is the warp of the weaving of experience, the threads that run the length of the fabric of our lives. The weft (woof), the fibers led by a shuttle in and out, over and under, through the weft/woof, are the whispers (and sometimes shouts) of possibility, of change, of opportunity. In the craft of weaving, a single line of fiber, a thread, drawn through the warp is called a pick. Pick by pick, change by change, a woven piece is built. The single pick does not reveal the ultimate design of the weaving. Only pick by pick, built one pass of the shuttle by another, reveals the nature of that which is being fabricated. It is a wonder to watch it evolve, pick by pick. Perhaps that divine whisper—the first whisper—is better understood as I watch and follow the designed possibles of the woof as they are woven into the strong, grounding consistency of the warp. Chaos and order are partners in creating growth and change. These things create and weave the fabric, the beautiful, functional, durable fabric that is our lives.

Is it time to become a partner to chaos and order to create growth and change?

Am I open-handed, clench-fisted, or reaching?

The most ergonomic and comfortable position is a resting, somewhat open hand. From this position, it's easy to move to a clenched fist or to reach for something. The resting open hand is the anatomical equivalent to Tae Kwon Do's ready stance, which is called Junbi. It is the start of everything in this martial arts discipline. I find the metaphorical comparison helpful. Clenching a fist becomes tiring. Reaching has the potential to throw someone off-balance. An open hand is ready: ready to start, ready to receive, to give, to deflect or defend. To approach a decision, a challenge, a day with an "open hand" allows the greatest level of immediate responsiveness. It is a physical manifestation of an inward attitude. Check your body, you'll notice if there is a clench present, a type of reach or an open resting hand.

What is your mental Junbi, your attitude of readiness? How do you recognize it is absent? How do you invite your courage to welcome a change in your day?

| # *Learn essential things by making irreverent inquiry.*

Consider asking yourself today...

"Are there essential things for you to learn using an irreverent inquiry?"

"Do you have long-cherished practices and beliefs that would serve you better if they were questioned irreverently?"

Has anyone ever said this to you? "That's not how we do things around here." If so, it's possible you were doing something outside the guardrails of their experience—off-track, at least from their perspective. The roots of this word reveal an action that does not revere or respect established norms or methods. Return again to the scientist. Using established testing protocols provides consistent results and generates a dependable baseline for comparison and measurement. It is the irreverent inquiry that elicits discovery, the *aha!* A quintessentially irreverent scientist, Albert Einstein, is credited with saying, "Doing the same thing over and over and expecting different results is insanity."

Irreverence is often mixed in with being disrespectful, and it certainly can be. An iconoclastic individual, a renegade of sorts, pushes against long-held or cherished beliefs. It's uncomfortable if you are the one holding tightly to the cherished beliefs that are being challenged. If you are the one forging uncharted waters, it can be both scary and exciting. Leaning into the positive aspects of irreverent questions means the possibility of a different than average result—an anticipated outcome. There's a familiar phrase often misattributed to Tony Robbins and many others—and if Henry Ford actually said it, he probably borrowed it from some older sage who borrowed it from the Stoics in his turn. That makes it an ancient understanding. "If you do what you have always done, you'll get what you've always gotten."

Can you brave the status quo and be irreverent in some way today?

60 | *Possibilities are seen more readily through a certain kind of lens.*

What frame are you looking through? There are microscopes and telescopes, magnifying glasses and eyeglasses, portals and windows. There are many ways—frames—to look at a thing. More important is recognizing that these different frames will allow one to see a variety of perspectives regarding one thing. Point of view is embodied in your choice of what frame to look through. This is true in:

- scientific evaluation
- metrics for bank loan decisions and academic considerations
- the way a participant is judged in a competition

Even what used to be called a beauty pageant is now considered more of a "scholarship" event. Yet still, it is driven by physical presence and appearance. One pageant judge may observe a competitor through the frame of culturally defined elements of beauty. Another judge might focus on poise, while still another may see through the frame of intellectual or innovative capacity. Everybody benefits when the observer is mindful of the frame which they have chosen to use. Even the one being observed benefits from knowing the type of evaluative frame that is being applied.

Paula Rudberg Lowe elaborates, *"The lens frames a person's expertise and experience. When forming a committee or board, it is vital to have people with various backgrounds to achieve a goal. Then create a structure: mission or focus, timeline, and goals. With that framework and the right people, the group can move forward. When people don't fit, it can stop or slow forward progress."*

Through what frames are you looking at your day?

61 | *Change likes to hide behind familiar things.*

It's not easy to know or notice if something (or anything) has changed. In a world where we consume so much that is already prepared for us, we can't always discern or are not always informed when something has been modified. We may not even know to ask until a previously dependable outcome shifts. This is relevant from relationships to restaurants, media content and literature, and from products to protocols.

I found a dog food Webster really liked. He's a finicky eater, and he liked this food a lot. It was a consistent acquisition, I purchased it from the same place regularly, and his mealtime and digestion were consistent. His disinterest in food arose over a week. After seven days of increasingly leaving food in his bowl, he ended up just leaving the food untouched. I took him to his vet. She had lots of questions after she evaluated him, including, "Has something—anything—changed?"

I assured her that there had been no change. The vet said that except for showing signs of hunger, Webster seemed perfectly fine. She disappeared out of the treatment room and came back with an open can of dog food and a bowl. She suggested an experiment. The bowl had been on the floor for approximately twenty-five seconds before it was eaten up, clean! Aha, it's the food. I was puzzled...my words trailed, "but it's been the same for..."

At home, I made a call to my food provider. They did some on-site research and they called the manufacturer. Turns out the company had reformulated that food product a few months earlier. Well, there it was. I found a new food and was schooled to remember to ask this question.

When predictable action suddenly delivers a different result, that is a clue worth your attention.

Is there a thread to follow leading to an identifiable "something" that has indeed changed?

Occasionally it requires getting lost in order to find your way.

You may reply to someone's observation, "Thank you, I've never looked at it that way before."

In the months before I started my greeting card company, I was creating installations for two fine art galleries and a wine shop: Large work, multimedia collage, and abstract watercolor paired with my poetry. The business owners took to explaining my works as "architectural collage" because I built so many layers into it. In retrospect, I might rather have called them engineered collage… But I distract myself—a form of getting lost!

My studio was the primary room in the house. My drafting table was flooded by natural light. One of my best pals would inevitably show up during my work hours, sometimes for a coffee break or cookie break, sometimes just for a chat. Regardless of the chosen exchange on a day, he, a student in the University of Oregon Department of Architecture, would turn whatever I was working on upside down and then say, "Now, finish it from here."

I am directionally dyslexic. If I feel as if I should take a right turn and I have the conscious awareness to do precisely the opposite, I will have actually taken the correct turn. My sense of direction is precisely 180 degrees counter to actual direction. That is how I began with my art, exactly upside down. I have learned proportion and balance over time. It took consistently turning my work upside down in order to gain the skills. Lynda Allen notes, *"In addition to upside down, there's also advantage to taking a step further away to see it from a distance."*

Will you be inspired to look at something from a different view this very day?

Will you turn it upside down, backward, or inside out and see what you learn?

63 | *Form the best question and then go to the right source.*

Who I decide to ask for feedback depends on the type of feedback I want to receive—or really, if I want feedback at all! How can I be prepared and open to receive the feedback, especially if it turns out to be something that disappoints me or something I really don't want to hear?

If I want or need structural feedback, I often turn to highly informed sources. These people demonstrate expertise in the field for which I require the feedback. I am looking essentially for an engineer in that area of interest. In this instance, the best source is an Engineer.

When I need strategic feedback, I require less tangible technical skill and more solid thinking skills. In fact, going to a good thinker, problem solver, and innovative out-of-the-box conceptualist gets results that are surprising. I often reach out to someone under the age of twelve. I find youngsters to be unfettered by the burden of knowing how things should be, and this allows them the capacity to candidly point out how things could be. At whatever age, people who think in this capacity are imagineers! For this need, an Imagineer is the ideal source.

If I just want feedback that is loving and supportive, I ask a friend who is informed not by technical skill or unconventional thinking but rather informed only by the accepting vision of how they see me. It is a rare opportunity to receive feedback from a source who connects to all three of these elements:

- the structural, the "what is" (an Engineer);
- the surprising, the "what if" (an Imagineer); and
- the supportive, the "what that will uplift" (a friend).

Who will you decide to go to for feedback when you have something you need to know?

64 | *Audacity is essential to imagine a small thing grown to its maximum potential.*

Most acorns do not make the journey to mature oak trees. Holding an acorn in one's hand, it is hard to imagine that it has the potential to stand sturdy as a mature oak one hundred years from that moment. Animals eat acorns, water soaks them, humans trample them and even consume them. There are many deterrents to an acorn growing fully into an oak tree. An acorn, by its very nature, contains the potential of becoming a mighty oak. In spite of seemingly insurmountable obstacles, many acorns actually do!

The potentials within any opportunity may seem so large as to make them exaggerated. Certainly it seems that way when holding an acorn and imagining a hundred-year-old oak tree. When confidence and imagination enlarge and expand, though, it is easier to view a very big potential as highly possible. Are there unimagined potentials yet waiting within your nature?

How can you expand your capacity to see a bigger potential?

65 If a choice is either medicine or poison, which is this?

Many conditions can be defined in high contrast terms. Rarely do dynamic systems stay in a neutral state: economy, health, blooming flowers. It's hard to imagine a life in which choices, any choice really, would be so severe. Yet there are situations on the planet where decisions do have this severe of a swing. My considerations are most often softer. It's easier on the nervous system to ask:

- Will this choice help or hinder?
- Will this choice heal or harm?

In context, this inquiry could be framed lots of ways, such as:

- Are these words I am about to speak going to delight or depress?

- Will the food I am about to consume build up my health or dip down my best efforts?

- Will taking this action align with a personal or greater goal or be outside of what I know are my priorities?

Professor Wallace Roarke calls this high contrast evaluation "other hand thinking." Few things in life remain in complete inactivity (stasis). Considering the choice by its extreme contrasts may support a quicker or clearer decision. A high contrast comparison can be helpful when two choices don't seem that distinctly different. When it's tempting to say of a choice, almost dismissively, "It doesn't matter," the idea of extending each choice to its opposite may make that choice clearer.

What if you consider a thing in the context of its severe opposite?

Courage doesn't always wait for every detail.

Sometimes courage chooses a door and walks right through it.

66 | *Imagine you have said yes. How does that feel?*

When faced with many opportunities, I use this question to imagine myself following more than one path. It initially narrows the choices and ultimately leads to a single choice that is backed by my enthusiasm and willingness.

Cheryl Craigie uses this question in a process she calls "conscious choice." She pays close attention to how she feels in the present moment when she imagines herself saying yes. If it feels right, even if it seems scary, she will commit and dive right in. That commitment enables her to fully embrace the experience or project. She notes that even in circumstances that are imposed on her rather than chosen, she searches for a way to offer her yes and choose her attitude moving forward. She summarizes her view with this: *"Life is so much better with the yeses."*

Yes can be an automated response fueled by a host of things. Yet a yes that can be fully embraced after careful consideration is a grace.

Are you clear on the delivery of your yes?

| # Pause long enough to consider the scope of your impact.

Who else might be impacted?

Can you expand your capacity to see a bigger circle of influence? When processing information for the sake of a decision, it's easy to feel as if both a decision and therefore, its consequence as well, are made in isolation. That is not always necessary. In asking who else may be involved in the impact or consequence, there's a balance to be found between giving too much consideration to the impact on others and not enough. Most people are familiar with the corporate adage that a camel is the result of a committee tasked with designing a horse. Considering impact must not imply assigning authority for the decision. It takes a high level of confidence to ask for feedback and solicit others' views on a thing. And it takes even more communication to be clear that you are not asking them to make a decision, but rather to contribute to your consideration of the matter. It's tempting for those in positions of authority to want to protect the impression that they know what they need to know. In reality, that is often not completely true. In the pause as you weigh the scope of your impact, consider also the benefit of seeking more views than simply yours alone.

How will you manage if you are you facing one of those kinds of decisions today?

You have choices. Yes; even not choosing is a choice. Perhaps you have said at some time, "I had to, I just had no choice." More accurately and said differently, it would be, "I could not see any alternative, and I felt compelled to make this decision."

Even selecting inaction, as opposed to the culturally familiar directive of "Don't just stand there, *do* something," is a choice. And often inaction is the valid choice.

The times are countless that I've been fussing and stewing over how I will intervene in a thing, while in the meantime, the thing resolves itself. Choices. Even identifying the most absurd or unlikely ones can lead to a choice that turns out to be ideal.

And choosing not to choose is...always a choice! Paula Rudberg Lowe explains that she likes to see all the options before she makes a choice, much like reading a menu. Sometimes she'll talk to a friend to see if they see more options that she hadn't thought of in the moment.

Jeanette Richardson Herring contributes this: *"Is it possible that you always have more choices than you can initially imagine? What's the alternative to the alternatives? There's always a choice, and if it appears there is none, no action can be the alternative. Often, for me, patience is the answer. What's most needed is on the way. Being observant is an answer, expecting to hear is an answer, I once heard the sweet whisper from Spirit. I never paint you into a corner—I always make a way of escape. Wait for it, breathe, wait for it."*

Can you simply identify some choices and pause on making any of them?

69 | *Do I need to establish or change my boundaries?*

There are natural boundaries that provide a clean, defined marking between here and there, this and that, outlining canyons, ridges, rivers, seas. These all create borders that people understand regardless of language or culture. There is not a sign required at any of these frontiers to insist that the traveler stop. It is not necessary.

Yet boundaries established in human relationships and cultural convention actually can require a sign of sorts.

If you've ever ordered a single dessert to share between two diners, you have likely created a defined boundary. It is divided into two pieces: one theirs, one yours. If your tablemate gobbles up their sweet real estate and starts in on your portion, you might be inclined to speak up. "Hey, I'm not done with that yet!"

A dessert cut into two distinct pieces is more measurable than a boundary of civility, of kindness, of agreement. The greater the clarity around human boundary, the greater the ease can be in speaking up when the boundary is crossed by accident or violated with intention.

How are you able to establish clear boundaries?

| **_Procrastination can be a signal for other sorts of underlying dynamics._**

"Let me think about that."

"Can I get back to you on that?"

Although procrastination manifests in multiple ways for diverse reasons, this consideration is for when a required and appropriate *no* masquerades as procrastination. Perhaps you've experienced this phenomenon on both sides of its equation.

You ask someone to volunteer for a committee position. They promise to get back to you. They don't. You ask again. Still thinking about it? More follow-up ensues. Chronic deferral can be taken as a decline. It is also a waste of time.

Maybe you have done it. You want to. You think you *ought*, yet you know you shouldn't. You just don't want to deliver a *no* to the person who has asked you. Postponing the decision only prolongs the pain and puts the person making the request in a tough spot. Procrastination can be an excellent litmus test through which to realize that an opportunity is not *your* opportunity. Procrastination is often the precursor to a more authentic answer.

Do you have a deferred decision that you will act on with your *no* today?

Is there a model that exists in the natural world for this?

The head of the entomology department was surprised at how much I, a non-academic, knew about the dragonfly. He was even more surprised when I outlined all the ways the dragonfly models systems of behavior for industry competition, marketing, branding, long-term planning, logistics, and systems management.

With an eye toward both transferable skills and the metaphorical, there are learning models to be found in every corner of the natural world.

Don't automatically eliminate that seemingly useless widget-whatcha-making too quickly. Consider the ubiquitous or apparently useless mosquito. But for their bites and itching, it's easy to assume they have no function in the world and wouldn't it be great to just toss them off the planet? After all, they carry disease and cause bites that inflame from irritation to pain. As I wrote decades ago, "Look again. Always look again."

Mosquitoes actually do some practically unseen pollinating. They are the primary food source of many insects, and in particular the dragonfly. A dragonfly will consume up to one hundred mosquitoes in a single day. If it were possible for you to give in to the impulse of eliminating mosquitoes from the face of the planet, you would be disrupting a fragile food chain, creating an organic crisis. Fortunately, it's not an impulse that too many people can act upon. Even a grand annoyance like the mosquito occupies an integral role in the larger scheme of things.

Is there a system from the natural world that you can model that would improve your experience?

72 | *Sometimes a distraction turns out to be the destination.*

I've notoriously borrowed a phrase from my wise friend, Kathleen. I use it so often people think it's original to me. The phrase?

"At a time that is not now."

Noticing something that needs doing while on your way to or engaged with something else becomes a distraction from your destination. It deserves attention, absolutely—just not your attention at that moment.

Not recognizing the difference turns your time into a Rube Goldberg machine. (Goldberg, a cartoonist and inventor, is known for creating complex mechanisms to achieve the simplest of actions.) Recall a time when you headed to a specific location in your home or office, and then hours later, you realized you hadn't completed what you first set out to do, but had done five other things…things that weren't even in your scope at the start of your day.

Jeanette Richardson Herring finds a middle place between distraction and destination: *"Maybe both. A distraction that becomes a destination, after all. There are days I need distraction from the*

And Sometimes It Does   101

daily-ness. Sometimes what seems distraction is a lovely interlude and can create a new destination. I might call that serendipity. Once I was distracted from my previous plan and ended up making a new friend."

The word distraction is formed from Latin roots which mean drag and apart. I want to keep that in mind if I am determining whether a thing is a distraction or not.

There are distractions that are known and predictable. They may even have a cute phrase to describe them like, "going down the rabbit hole." Social media deservedly has the reputation of readily becoming a distraction (a rabbit hole), and it is by design. Media platforms are intentionally built to be irresistible in all possible ways.

How does one tell the difference between a distraction and, say, an opportunity or a necessity? First, not all things that distract are distractions. That's the beauty of setting a timer. I will give myself over to a craft and set an alarm for when I need to turn the metaphorical "simmering soup" off. When the timer beeps, I am distracted from what I am doing, yes. However, it is not a distraction but a determined necessity. If, while I am turning the heat off under the soup pot, I notice I've left the spices out and then return them to the spice cupboard only to notice they have fallen off their spice shelves… And then I decide to reorganize and noticed the spices have dusted the shelves and perhaps I should take them all out and wipe down the shelves… You've already guessed where this is going. That is indeed a distraction. When a thing not of necessity takes you from what you said matters most in the moment, it may qualify as a distraction. To

Courage Doesn't Always Roar...

the etymology of it, it drags you apart from your priorities. When you suddenly pivot, ask: destination or distraction?

Is this for now or for a time that is not now?

73 | *Every single decision has brought you to this very moment.*

The conversation around the training table had become increasingly tense. Participants had begun reflecting on various poor decisions in their past, and it quickly moved to levels of anxiety about the future. Sentences beginning with "what if" populated the air:

- What if I make an incorrect order?
- What if I proposed an incorrect procedure?
- What if my decision unintentionally stalls progress?

The quietest participant spoke up. With five words, Caren Albers changed the trajectory of the exchanges. She did not ask a question but made a statement: "There are no wrong turns."

These words stacked up every judgment about previous decisions and their consequences like we were watercraft and they were the wind that blew us there. They did. Everything about our past has brought us to this present moment. If you are content with who you see in the mirror, then perhaps you can find a way to accept every turn that brought you to this place.

Can you reframe the idea of a wrong turn into just a turn?

Is the expenditure available, justifiable, refundable?

In business and personal finance, there are diverse expenses that are predictable and there are some expenses that are completely unexpected. I've certainly been caught short in both business and personal finances.

Available: The question of the funds for the expenditure being available is very important. As recently as a completely unexpected cross-country trip, the necessity of a "just in case" category in my budget process was shown to be essential, mandatory. If funds are available in a set-aside fund for emergencies and the expenditure is not an emergency, then the answer to the question is no, the funds are not available. The other aspect to this question involves the thing itself—the expenditure. There are times in real estate, for example, where a deal is snagged before you can even call your realtor. Or a one-of-a-kind object that you decided to think about for a while is no longer available. Poof. Gone.

Justifiable: The first inquiry in this category is to ask if a justification is actually required. It is? Then these questions are helpful:

- Is it necessary?
- Is it helpful?
- Does it align with what matters most?

Refundable: There are times when even with a 100 percent sense of confidence regarding a particular acquisition or expenditure, returning the thing becomes necessary. Having the information as to whether it is refundable or returnable may more fully inform your decision. Some expenditures have more inherent risk in the making. These considerations may clarify.

Which of these questions seems most relevant to you today? How can you apply it to your circumstances?

75 | *At first, it may appear there are no options. Always look again.*

One of the most paralyzing circumstances is when I feel as if I have no choice in a matter. Options, or the awareness that I can seek out options, are essential to my personal agency and sense of equanimity. Having that confidence in a circumstance emboldens my capacity.

In a circumstance that feels restrictive at best, I use my imagination. I take a deep breath with a long exhale and imagine myself, some amount of time away from now, in a place that is spacious and full of choices. In my imagination, I picture myself independent, completely absent any restrictive circumstances. I view that future me from several vantage points. Then I follow threads backward. How did that future me make it to that place apart from the current restriction? This visualization allows me to identify choices which were not immediately evident even in the moments just before. Voila! Options. The imaginary exercise provides another benefit. It reminds my body to remember what it feels like to be in choice. My shoulders release their proximity to my ear lobes in that remembering!

What system do you effectively employ to identify your viable options in the face of a restrictive circumstance?

76 | *There are structures to be found even in things that appear random.*

I am fond of the organic organizing systems found within seemingly random structures. Randomness oddly crafts a balance. It is as if the universe conspires to present an elegant and orderly result from apparent chaos.

As a lifelong planner, it is odd that I am so fond of creating beauty from random bits, finding meaning within principles and structures that appear arbitrary. I recognize circumstances frequently demand I relinquish my comfort with and desire for control. In these instances of willingness and openness, I am able to appreciate the value of welcoming that which is random.

Is it possible to find a fortuitous structure in things that may seem incidental?

Does this align with the fire of my intentions?

The body knows when an activity aligns with the fire of an intense, deeply held intention. It warms. It lights up. It shows the way. When an action or event is out of alignment with the fire of intention, the body knows.

When a task, activity, or exchange is off-kilter and unaligned, it has a weight to it. Modern life and the variety of demands in a single day can create a disconnect between the truth of our experience and our bodies, how our bodies register and manifest that truth, and how unfortunately we frequently cognitively override our own intuition and body-knowing. Susan Knezel Reardon, educator and runner, expands: *"What this means for me today is slow down. Slower. Even slower. Nope, still not slow enough. Find my body's pace #RunningIsAMetaphorForEverything."*

Is there alignment in your choices today? Listen to what your body will tell you.

In what way can you be more connected to the messages your body delivers to you?

Will this accommodate my most significant deficit or my obvious vulnerability?

As pendulums swing, so do our deficits and vulnerabilities. It takes courage in the first place to show the soft underbelly of your deficit or apparent weakness. Madeline L'Engle, author of *A Wrinkle in Time*, has her character, Meg, learn in a profound way that it was now to her faults she had to turn in order to save herself.

My depth of feeling is one of my greatest vulnerabilities. It makes me susceptible to being taken advantage of. It inclines me toward inappropriately hurt feelings. It also fuels my writing career with emotive poetry and profoundly empathetic writings on my product offerings. It allows me to gently mirror the experiences of my clients and friends.

Perhaps you are very aware of the things within you that are traditionally considered deficits. As you might make a list, draw a line to the opposite quality of what you identify. It's very likely that the strength represented in that thread doesn't get the attention it deserves.

Can you leverage what shows up as a discernible deficit into being used as a tool of strength?

Pause at the gate of your strongly held view to consider something new.

A long-time friend and trusted advisor came to stay for five days. Her decorative and organizational skills are magnificent. I put my living room in her hands without reservation, with one exception. There was a single piece of furniture I was ready to jettison. I had tried it in many different configurations, and none of them worked. With each unsuccessful placement, my resistance to the piece increased. I offered unqualified trust for her skill with the one caveat that "This particular piece has to go."

Early in her redesign, she asked if I would consider keeping it. No, I would not. I was past considering. My mind was set. A few hours later, she asked again—and yet again. The fourth time she asked me, she framed it in this way, "I know you have strong feelings about this furnishing. I really think it has potential, and would you consider letting me try it out in this specific place?" I called to mind the trust I felt for her friendship and skill set. I set aside my strongly held opinion. I allowed myself to consider.

Now it's a wonderful and intrinsic part of my reconfigured living room.

What strong opinion may you set aside today in order to consider something new?

| ## *Is the effort too large for my single reach?*

Consider two perspectives at play in this question. The first is that everything is possible, and independently, that any effort is achievable. The other view is to dream big and ask for help building a ladder that will reach the apex of the aspiration.

It's one thing to experience personal doubt about the capacity to implement a momentous project. The power of our desire to complete a reach is consistently underestimated. Recognize the value of the effort. That recognition enables the dreamer to do what is necessary and enlist the help of others. It's been said by so many over the decades. I hear Hillary Clinton, enunciating clearly, "We are stronger together."

It takes some gumption to ask for assistance in reaching a dream. Think about the opportunity that you are generating for those who are being asked: You are modeling having the grit to ask for help. It's possible you will inspire others to do the same.

Do you need to find some capable and willing others with whom to work together? How?

8 | *It is the brave soul who willingly integrates who they are with how they speak and what they do.*

The concept and practice of setting priorities is tossed about in many layers of exchange, both in personal life and business. There is what we *say* is important. That's usually represented by some sort of list.

There's what we *do* in a day. That's usually driven by what actually matters in the moment. Sometimes the *doing* unfolds purely as reaction, responding to drama, the unexpected, and other people's priorities gone awry.

When what we *say* and *do* align, there is power, momentum, and reward. When they are contrary to each other, there's ennui, discomfort, and a feeling that something is not quite right.

If you are not moving your existing priorities forward on a daily basis, do you need to reconsider what matters to you? Do you have the personal chutzpah to be present in the world with all aspects of yourself in alignment?

If you are unclear on your priorities for the day, do you need to authenticate what matters most?

82 | *Be unceasingly creative. It is the truest way to discovery.*

It happens when what the recipe calls for isn't anywhere around. Then you ask, what else might work? Will something else do? Someone might say to you, "I never would have thought of doing it that way." And you might answer, "Me neither. But I needed to finish, and I didn't have the right ingredient/thing/part."

Thinking of fresh applications for old tools and familiar materials and outdated ideas is a sure way to discovery, just as getting lost inevitably helps you find something useful you didn't know was available.

How do you sustain your creativity?

83 | *Will this root me or uproot me?*

It is tempting to associate being uprooted with something undesirable or uncomfortable. A bonsai is purposely never uprooted. It remains rooted to a small pot, trained to be restrained and small. Bonsai is an ancient practice. It is beautiful. It realizes one kind of aesthetic, one kind of beauty that does not involve allowing the tree to deepen its roots and grow unfettered.

City planners often plant a landmass for the immediate impact, not considering the long term. The strip of soil, grass, or rock between the sidewalk and the street becomes problematic in many planned urban areas. There are rows of trees that looked pristine in the 1960s and were majestic in the 1980s; then fast-forward some decades to the present, and the root systems of their unrestrained growth break the cement, imperil water pipes, and create pedestrian hazards with the irregular angles of the sidewalk. The deepened roots exceed their context.

This question invites the risk/cost benefit analysis of a thing in a more imaginative and consequential way.

Are you rooting into a thing or being willingly uprooted?

84 | *If there are obstacles, there are systems available for identifying them.*

We are collectively so accustomed to the (uniquely American) myth that we must fight for everything of value that encountering no resistance is a surprising thought. It's possible that the path to acting on a specific impulse may encounter no obstacles. Experience, however, allows that there will likely be obstacles along the way. Some obstacles are so unique that they dwell beyond the capacity to imagine them—I never saw that one coming! Providing a litany of potential obstacles in advance is a sure way to support the deferral of a dream.

What if courage pairs up with your specific desire to move a dream forward? Courage might consistently whisper, "Perhaps there will be obstacles. We will face them together as we encounter them."

What might your journey look like with courage on your travel team?

What doors might you walk through if you considered them as thresholds instead?

85 | *It takes effort to avoid seeing only what we think we are looking for.*

Are we objective? My quick answer to this question is no. Not only am I not objective, I have to work diligently to not be entirely subjective! Humans are an amalgam of all their experiences and bits or volumes of knowledge. All of that conspires to create a bias unique to each individual. Unintentionally, humans naturally seek information in situations that confirm their biases, a phenomenon called confirmation bias. Such seeking and finding provides a comforting level of knowing and ease. Intentionally creating a system of inquiry promotes the capacity to ask a broad range of questions.

How would I proceed if I were remarkably objective on this issue? How would I advise someone to proceed on a matter for which I was reasonably objective?

These questions can lift you out of your unique bias, if only a little. You can use focus groups, research, a pro and con list, and various forms of checklists, as well as asking for the views of disinterested parties (who will have a subjective view that is at least different than yours!). All of these are steps toward not simply seeing what you were expecting to see.

In what ways can you reach for a more significant objectivity in a matter today?

86 | *Sometimes when you are scared, there is a justifiable reason.*

It doesn't matter whether the reason you are scared is justified. Facing the feeling of being scared deserves courageous attention, regardless of the reason. *Scared* is the nameplate on the door of many extraordinary opportunities. It is also the barely heard whisper acting as your dear friend requesting, "Please practice in quieter waters first before taking your first kayak journey ever in your life in white water rapids."

Being scared of venturing into a new thing is often a perfect time to pause. Pause and take stock, look around, make assessments. Scared is the soundtrack that often plays right before the big moment in the movie comes along. That moment can involve either moving forward into the scary thing or catching sight of the back of your jacket as you decide to walk away. Either direction constitutes a "big moment" in the movie that plays out as your life.

It's a paradox that the partner to courage is the capacity to understand and acknowledge being scared.

Is it possible to use the feeling of being scared to your advantage?

87 | *Is there space for allowing magic?*

What is magic if not utterly surprising and completely unanticipated? Magic is something seemingly without rational explanation. A magic moment can appear anywhere, at any time. In fact, magic is happening all around us all of the time. The thing is, magic has to be noticed, and we need to be willing to see it.

The other day, I was disappointed to learn the right plants for my garden in order to attract dragonflies were not available at my nursery of choice. Additionally, I had priced lots of different water features, a known favorite of the dragonfly, but had decided they all exceeded my budget and bumped up against my conservation approach to water usage. Just two days after that decision, which sounded a lot like *no*, I received a *big magic Yes* from a dragonfly swarm. They circled and darted and flew around my tiny patio garden. It was magical! The dragonfly community themselves had made space for magic. I noticed.

Additionally, my immediate community made space for magic by realizing a long-held aspiration of a large water feature on our shared property. The dragonflies are happy, and so am I.

What unanticipated whimsey will you allow to walk into your day?

88 | *There seems to be a right season for everything.*

"This is my season" isn't a catchy phrase, but it is rich in meaning. It's an acknowledgment that you are living to the edge of your possibilities at this particular time.

In her classic work *Passages*, published in 1974, Gail Sheehy identifies the seasons of life by the types of challenges that are faced in various stages of a person's years. It is common to correlate the spring season to a young person. Equally familiar is saying an elder is in the autumn or the winter of their life. It's a concept that has helped countless people understand the progression of their life experiences. Kathleen is a registered nurse who is also trained in many alternative modalities. She helped me craft a more spacious living space by identifying which of my many souvenirs and meaningful objects were appropriate for a particular season. I sorted objects of meaning and beauty into four different storage bins and began the process of trading them out according to each season. It focused my space, provided a meaningful seasonal transition, and gave my meaningful objects more of an opportunity to be seen and truly appreciated.

Beyond how it can apply to objects, the concept of seasonal relevance applies to food choices, color, and types of clothing, activities and movements, and even what a body requires for a sense of wellness. Adhering to the progression of the seasons in a calendar year connects us to ancestral heritage and a sense of genetic disposition in aligning with the demands and benefits of each different season.

Susan Knezel Reardon writes, *"I am all about owning my autumn right now. Autumn is more spare and stripped down—it's the season that has let a lot of stuff go. But it has its own uniquely spectacular beauty and its own gifts. Knowing that winter is around the corner gives it some sense of purpose too—do what you want to or need to do before hibernation time comes."*

A season. What is yours on this day?

89 | *Be relentlessly curious.*

The reminder to be relentlessly curious comes naturally to many people. I am a curious person, and I love research. I am able to identify two consistent experiences when I do not demonstrate a measurable curiosity. When a friend is vulnerable and disclosing intimate details of a struggle, I often resist the urge to make a deeper inquiry. When someone says to me that yesterday was really hard for them and would I hold a good thought for them, I do not succumb to the urge to ask any version of why or exactly what happened. In that situation, I believe they would tell me if they wanted me to know. Perhaps I will occasionally ask, "Is there anything else you want me to know about this?" Knowing that I am curious, someone will be surprised when they ask me more information about a mutual friend and I reply that I don't know. The inquiry then turns to didn't you ask? And my response always is that they didn't offer the information.

Courage Doesn't Always Roar...

The other circumstance is when my feelings are hurt. Even though I work to dismantle my set of triggers, I take things too personally. When I become embroiled in hurt, with what curiosity I can muster, I'm usually wondering what it is that I have done wrong. That is as far as my curiosity can travel when I am hurt. At a time when I can connect to the objective, effective tool of curiosity, I am able to respond to that inclination with the grand question, "What else might be true?" That inquiry helps invite curiosity in an area where I resist it.

Do you know where your best curiosity dwells? Are you aware in what circumstances you resist being curious?

90 | *Be here. Be present to this now.*

My body has a clear and consistent signal for when my mind is not in the same place as my feet. It is evident in the fact that I bump into things; or I trip. When I am present to my surroundings, here, and mindful of the moment, now, my body honors physical borders and boundaries and navigates every path, place, or road with a certain grace.

Ram Dass brought the phrase into the global cultural awareness in the early 1970s with his book, *Be Here Now*. Paul Wesselmann, author and speaker, uses these two words (Here and Now) as his personal grounding mantra and often opens a keynote with these two words as an effective invitation to his audience. Dr. Deanna Davis quips, "Be here, now. Be there, then."

I consider it an invitation for myself, an audience of one, to the best kind of party, one where a buffet of awareness, contentment, and flow is endlessly available.

How can you tell when you are completely engaged with the present moment?

91 | *Have the courage to show your dreams to the world.*

"Yeah, but you said you were going to…"

Have you had a time when you were judged or measured against the dream you spoke aloud? Perhaps you encountered levels of pushback because the specific outcome didn't materialize?

It takes courage to show your dreams to the world. Speaking out about a deeply held aspiration creates an implied accountability. Even if you didn't *ask* for accountability, undoubtedly, somebody's going to deliver it to you. Someone will remind you, even shame you, about the thing you said you wanted to do and then didn't do. Makes you want to repeat, "Walk on by, nothing to see here."

I've been showing my dreams to the world since I was a kid. Lots of them have become real. Others still dwell entirely in my imagination. And others languish in a field of not-to-be dreams. I dreamed of helping liberate the attitudes of those imprisoned by actual barbed-wired walls by teaching writing practices. I said it out loud. I took consistent action toward it, and it took almost sixty months before I actually walked through a prison door to teach writing practices, but I did. I continued to act on that dream for as long as it took me to make it come true.

Pam Williams disclosed to me, *"I anticipate that sometime later this year I will begin saying some of my dreams out loud to my world. I will ask myself to welcome accountability and people who want to believe in my dreams along with me."*

Saying and showing my dreams to the world brings a stability to the road that walks me toward a realized dream.

Can you say out loud even a small part of a big dream?

92 | *Our body confirms correct decisions and tries to tell us.*

When relief floods my belly, when my shoulders drop and my jaw unclenches, I know that saying *no* was the correct choice. There are many motivations behind saying no, and not all of them feel great. In some instances, the body telegraphs the answer that connects to our truest intentions. That might mean experiencing regret over declining an opportunity. In an unpublished poem, poet Susan Knezel Reardon writes of self-soothing and how her body interprets a correct statement: *"...this muddy Creekside patch. This place where gnarled roots insist on mindfulness, favorite path littered with memories of poems born right here on previous paths through these trees. I am a poet. We translate the body's message."*

Translating the body's message is a significant decision-making skill. Bessel van der Kolk, a psychiatrist specializing in the processing of trauma, underscores scientifically that the body knows the truth of a thing, and in fact remembers it by storing it at a cellular level. With this knowledge of the visceral response given to a thing, a delivered *no* allows an individual's awareness to rise. Imagining a delivered *no* will tip the direction of a decision. Giving the actual *no* and then attentively observing the consequences in your body serves as either confirmation or an invitation to reconsider.

How can you listen if your body is sending you a message today?

93 | *Risk likes to show up at parties wearing different costumes.*

All kinds of roads have guardrails. They are a visual indicator, a reminder of the most practical way to propel the hundreds of pounds of metal you are in. They are a physical barrier returning you to the road should you accidentally veer their way. They are a retainer, meant to slow or minimize your harm should you barrel through them. What of the time when you observe a thing, an object, a stranded animal, a person in need, an alluring path? All things on the other side of the guardrail?

That is a question that becomes a narrative of risk. At the side of the road, in a seat at a boardroom table, in the middle of a stock trade, in silence before you speak or in those seconds when your finger lingers over the "send" button, these are experiences of risk being questioned, considered, weighed.

Is what I am about to do or what I am thinking of doing *worth* what I may sacrifice, what I may give up in order to reach for this?

Can you recognize it, and how will you ask if a thing is worth the risk?

94 | *Clarity comes when you assign an immediacy to a decision.*

If I had to decide and resolve this right now, what next action would I take? That phrase I learned from Kathleen, "at a time that is not now," has been used for years to very good advantage. It is not a procrastination device so much as a deferral and a recognition of priority. It acknowledges that whatever the consideration is does not exceed the priority of what I am already doing. It is important, and it will get to be fully tended at another time. Not now.

What of the decisions that cannot bear postponement? Or what about issues that repetitively present themselves on which you simply have no clarity regarding the choice of this or that? "Let's flip a coin," isn't such a copout as some might think. A coin toss, the odds of which aren't quite 50/50, does several different things in the process of a decision.

In their book *The Leading Brain*, Fabritius and Hagemann make the point that a coin toss reveals a person's actual leaning. It unveils the decision an individual has at some deeper level already made, but can't consciously access. How is this done? By observing your reaction to the result of the toss. After value is assigned to heads or tails and the coin is tossed, the individual evaluates their response. If they are relieved, they then go with the decision. Slightly disappointed? With that disappointment, it is more likely that your better choice is the alternative. They point out this is a great way to access deeper intuition that has consciously eluded you.

Researchers, University of Chicago scientists among them, have identified a different value in the coin toss. They suggest an unclear choice is often rooted in a resistance to shouldering responsibility for the outcome. In situations where personal responsibility isn't necessary or required—as in, should we order takeout from the Chinese restaurant down the street or from the pizza joint?—there is measurable relief in allowing a coin toss to arbitrate that choice. Various researchers found people were happier with the outcome when it was removed from their own personal responsibility. There are at least two ways to look at making a decision in the present moment. Want to toss a coin for which one you'll use today?

Sue Robson has seen this woven through her life as a lay minister and the lives of those very dear to her. She elaborates, *"To be responsible for the decision one makes will at times stop the decision from being made. Thus, nothing may get done. Movement forward will stall, options become limited, and what 'may come to be' will never be known because of the fear of being responsible for the outcome. What if the outcome is glorious but it never manifests due to this fear? Ahhhh... May we act as if the Good will be revealed as we take the steps needed to move into the direction that is best, versus staying where we are never knowing the joy we chose not to pursue."*

Will you try tossing a coin to see if you can clarify your decision?

95 | *What if I pretended everything was easy?*

I navigated most of my childhood through poetry, journal writing, and my imagination. Two questions I often used were, "What if I pretended everything was easy?" and, "Imagine how it would be if I knew how to do this."

Elizabeth Drewry Beck notes, *"I have something today that I am worried is going to be hard...But I am changing my mind...I am going to pretend it is easy...Which seems easier than worrying about it ahead of time."*

Most children use imagination for flights of fancy or a retreat from reality. I had books for that! Imagination, rather than a retreat from actual life, was my door to operating in real life in some capacity and/or range that fit the norms. It was a necessary tool growing up. As an entrepreneur in my adult life, the practice has transferred well.

"Managerial imagination" is a thing. It's a practice allowing professionals, particularly human resource executives, to challenge assumptions about their organization and to preemptively anticipate issues among their workforce. As a professional practice, managerial imagination allows these people to be more immediately responsive when a previously anticipated problem actually arises. Those business-y folks at Harvard School of Business suggest that employing unfettered imagination is a practical way to elevate strategic thinking. In the past, planning used to be chastised with the conservative admonition, "Now, don't go letting your imagination get too wild." But in recent times, it's evident that an unfettered imagination is an invitation to ideas that may seem absurd on the surface and yet lead to unexpectedly innovative actions or solutions. How might this day be different if you untethered your imagination and let it fly around your whole day?

What can you imagine is easy today?

96 | Explore the expansiveness of an idea and make room for it in the day.

I should write that down so I don't forget it.

I'm sure I'll remember this amazing idea in the morning...

If only I wasn't so busy right this moment, I'd like to do some research on that.

Some of the Best Ideas never get through the door, even though they knock a really long time. "Come back later. I'm really busy right now." And then, if your experience resembles mine, a week or so later, you may have a vague recollection of what that idea was. However, the memory is so vague that it just doesn't spark any particular action. In a clear effort toward focus and diligence, ideas are often disregarded. Even with genuine and valuable ideas, I mistakenly believe that I will remember to get to them later. Many laters later, I end up losing even the loosest connecting thread.

A planning system I created a long time ago has a card in it titled, "flashes of brilliance for a time that is not now." Making room for an idea in your day does not require that you drop every single plan and wholeheartedly expand on that particular potential. It can be as respectful as a note in your journal or on a post-it.

With the presence of so many digital assistants, it can be waking an AI system and asking it to remind you at a later time of this great idea (Hey, Siri, Alexa! Hey, google). Ideally, the reminder will be for some time relatively soon. This is an excellent idea for Ideators, who travel life with myriad ideas in a single day. For those who observe a strategically planned task day, knowing when to shift out of a plan and make room for wondering can be the key to a keen discovery. Conversely, those chronically distracted by a steady stream of great ideas will benefit from the discipline of making note for a later time. Brilliant structures emerge from that pivotal moment when you allow your head to turn from your predicted tasks, recognizing, "*This*! This might really expand into a great idea with an amazing, impactful outcome," and then? Remember to remember it!

In what way will you acknowledge your flashes of brilliance that are for a time yet to come?

97 | *Map out the options.*

"I don't know what to do."

I will say this to myself, and then, I invite myself to look and consider all that I could do. Before I do that, before the mapping of options begins, I determine if there is a specific or even a general outcome or direction that I ultimately want. If I am also unsure of where I want to end up, I get ready for some discovery—and surprise. This activity is largely imaginative and speculative, as is any venture into a supposed future. The most significant result of mapping out options is that I lift the curtain on my own actual preferences. Essentially, I can find out where I want to go or what I want to do by first uncovering what I do not want. I've named this the "Goldilocks Razor." As a reminder, a conceptual razor is a rule-of-thumb guiding principle that shaves off other considerations, ultimately just leaving one. Goldilocks Razor is a purposeful redundancy. In the tale, Goldilocks goes through the repetitive process of eliminating undesirable or less-than-ideal options (too hot, too cold), until she gets to the one that is "just right." When one operates within a community, it takes some fortitude to speak up on behalf of what is just right for you.

A map is a visual representation of an area showing its various features. It is helpful to map out options when it is not obvious how to get from one point to another. This isn't a metaphorical exercise. It is a means of diagramming graphically where you might want to go and be. When I was mapping out my options between being an employee, with a presumed level of security and a steady paycheck, and starting my own greeting card business, which I considered risky (especially without start-up capital), I wrote, *"The jump is so frightening between where I am and where I want to be. Because of all I may become, I will close my eyes and leap."* That mapping of options delivered an unanticipated insight. Being an employee is not really the more secure option. The circumstance of employment exists alongside the person with the authority to fire me. Launching into what looked like the riskier route ultimately delivered greater personal agency and authority over my own life.

Mapping out options brings unimagined clarity. In the process of doing so, I move from the space of "I don't know what to do" to a level of informed enthusiasm and readiness to take the first step in the general direction of my ultimate hope or dream. Readiness need not employ immediate action. Sometimes the clarity of direction affirms a practical pause. You never know until the options are mapped out!

What is a first step toward applying the Goldilocks Razor to determine what is just right for you?

98 | *Consider the costs.*

Only you know the potential costs of what you are thinking of undertaking. You know the systems necessary to identify them. You know the practices to flush them out. Have the guts to tell yourself the bone truth—you know some of the costs, and you also know there are some risks and consequences you cannot even begin to imagine.

No. Yes.

Both answers require a level of courage.

That fence you've been sitting on? It's time…

Consider the cost and decide.

99 | *Will there be another opportunity like this?*

You can never really know the answer to this question. This inquiry is based in an unknowable future, and to answer it is purely speculative.

So what does asking this question actually do? It puts any consideration in context. Recognizing the most accurate way to answer this question is *no* puts the potential before you in a greater spotlight. If you will never get this opportunity again, can you reconcile yourself to passing it by? Will you gamble on the potential of seeing it again? Does it match up with what you say matters most to you? That's the real bell ringer. If it does not have an alignment with your core intentions, perhaps that makes it easier to pass a "once in a lifetime opportunity" by.

How do you evaluate what opportunities to seize and when to seize them?

*Courage cannot know
the outcome from
a single action.*

*It can quietly assure
that kindness is never
a poor choice.*

100 | *If kindness had a family tree...*

Kindness is sibling to Surprise, Giving, and Legacy. Her parents are Mercy and Presence. Her maternal grandparents are Equanimity and Compassion. Her paternal grandparents are Equality and Equity. Her daughter is Acceptance. Acceptance learned from Kindness that all the songs of the celestial choir are hers to sing. She never needed to ask for them, insist upon them, or demand them—they were always hers, hers to receive. Kindness is a member of a larger family known for standing for justice, hospitality, and generosity and for comfortably sitting at a table large enough for everyone.

Where on your family tree of qualities does kindness show up?

101 | *There are many ways to express the path forward.*

I smile regardless of the context in which I hear the word "forward." In business and industry-related documentation, it will be used to define momentum. It calls up something different, however, for me.

We did enjoy each other's company. These two men had been together since they were so young. When the legal status of marriage expanded to include their love and commitment, I stood with them and hosted their celebratory reception.

On occasions when I drove on our adventures, they gradually trained my vocabulary. Instead of asking, "Do I go straight or do I turn?" they trained me to ask, "Do I go forward here?" Yes, forward, not straight.

What this one-directional word informs us of is the power of language to include or exclude. These men grew up in a period of time where there was a single measure of correct humanity, being "straight": straight, not gay. Forward offers concise and encompassing guidance. Straight is fraught with judgment and disempowerment. Language can be nuanced, and it is also, in many instances, not subtle. Words matter.

Look at your language and ask if it is inclusive.

How can you move forward with words that offer kindness, grace, and dignity?

102 | *Allow your generosity to enlarge the world.*

Everyone's impulse toward and definition of generosity is different. I remind myself often that I do not give because I have extra, I give because I have enough.

Generosity is expansive. One generous act often calls forth another, in both the giver and the recipient. Think of the driver who pays the ferry toll for the car behind them or the long train of coffee purchases passed along in the drive-through line. Spontaneous and

Courage Doesn't Always Roar...

therefore utterly unexpected acts of generosity are breathtaking and live long in the memory.

A distraught dog owner took a photo of their missing canine to a business center. They were dismayed to learn that design services were no longer available, only duplication of existing designs. My friend Barbara Frank, a computer design whiz who was in line behind the person looking for their lost dog, immediately offered to design the poster for them. They stepped over to an on-site computer and got the poster done. Her generosity enlarged the world of one human and, one can hope, the missing dog's world as well.

In what way can you allow generosity to be present in your day either as the giver or the receiver?

103 | *Let your own listening be intense. Model the behavior you want to inspire in others.*

As the color blue goes, there is a soft robin's egg blue, and then there's the intense blue that is the color of a blueberry. That color is assessed as the most intense color in the world. There are lots of blues, and they are certainly not the same.

"I already told you this, weren't you listening?" Have you heard this or said it? Is there a sting associated with this feeling of being unseen or forgotten?

I see you.

It's a comforting phrase; beloveds and colleagues alike understand it to mean myriad things:

- I accept you.
- I love you as you are.
- You belong; and perhaps most significantly,
- I hear you because I pay attention to you.

I am touched when a friend recalls a small but important detail from a conversation from years gone by. I am affirmed when a colleague translates what I've just said into their own words as a demonstration that they have understood.

Be the rich, intense and memorable color of blueberry in your listening to others. Deep listening perpetuates the behavior in others. And when it doesn't inspire that behavior in another? That's free data that the non-listener is providing you. Pay attention.

Will you notice how you listen and who listens intensely to you?

104 | *Attentiveness is an essential element of successful endeavors and relationships.*

Perhaps you can recall a time as a student when a teacher said, "Attention! Give me your undivided attention!" It was required to at least look as if you were paying attention. As adults, many people continue the practice of halfheartedly looking as if they are paying attention...

Attention is:

- The ultimate efficiency hack. When you are attentive to something, it requires less repetition and it increases your grasp and understanding of it.

- The quintessential safety skill. When navigating a walking path, driving, or operating equipment of any sort, your level of attention elevates the likelihood of your safety.

- An essential ingredient in relating with others. The magical ease in any relationship is paved with consistent or undivided attention. In this context, there is no device in hand, no scrolling screens nor other reading material that is blocking eye contact. The device is put down. The book is set aside. The television is turned off, or at least set to mute. To give another human (or an event or effort) your full attention is an investment in the longevity of that exchange.

What are additional benefits of attention?

Which benefit of attentiveness will you employ today?

105 | *Engage with the same level of wonder as a child.*

When a client needs a shot of creativity, requires a bump or volley in their capacity for play, or would benefit from anything to elevate their curiosity, I encourage them to seek out experts in these arenas. Just about any four- or five-year-old will do. Absent the availability of a child, I suggest that a terrier is an excellent alternative; or really, almost any dog. The wonder that is housed in the spirit of a very young child or an animal is extraordinary.

Wonder is the feeling of surprise mingled with admiration, and it is caused by something beautiful, unexpected, or inexplicable. In adults, this quality is known as awe. It is often associated with being captivated by something like a view of the Grand Canyon or a remarkably decorated multilayered birthday cake! A child doesn't require a thing to be one of the seven wonders of the world in order to be in awe of it: A frog, a colorful bird, a wrapped gift, the box the gift came in, a piece of mail addressed to them…all merit the wonder of a child. The wonder of a child manages to always put the extra into the ordinary.

What would be different for you today if you engaged with a child's level of wonder?

106 | *Esperanza is Spanish for hope.*

I consider hope an excellent alternative to expectations. Expectations are sneaky things, have pointy parts, and often pal around with regret and disappointment.

I can think of many parties at which I was on the cusp of feeling hope for gracious outcomes. And wouldn't you know that expectation comes sauntering over and starts complaining about the food table. Apparently, says expectation, the host didn't know that there were guests who actually enjoy cheeses and meats. "It looks as if it's a guest list filled with vegans!" expectation says disparagingly. Expectation expresses dissatisfaction about the music, both the selections and the volume. Additional commentary comes on the subject of the poor seating arrangements. I interrupt and feebly offer that I was hopeful to see some very old friends. Then I excuse myself quickly, saying that I'd spotted one of them!

Hope and hopefulness: That story is a metaphorical example of how expectations sneak up on me. The snarky tone is a clear indicator that expectations, whether legitimate or not, are held and being failed.

Emily Dickinson said hope is the thing with wings. Maybe that's because hope can lift one above the severe clutches of specific and often unfounded expectations.

Will you check yourself today, whether you are experiencing hope or expectation? How?

107 | *Dance a little and try again.*

She told me she thought I was one of the bravest people she knew. *Brave in what way?* you might wonder. Did I save some lives in San Francisco? Nope. Did I rush oncoming traffic to rescue a lost pet? Nope. What did I do? I led a congregation in worship with dance for which I had no training and only moderate talent. What did I have?

A leotard and tights, a love for dance, and an adoring relationship with God. I knew from the biblical account that David, also not a professional dancer, danced, and the Lord was made happy. So, I danced. Sure, there were those who observed with judgment that my legs were less than trim and my stout body was poured into a black long-sleeve leotard. Then there were those who were inspired by comparison, saying to themselves: "If she can do *that*, then I can certainly do *this*..."

I danced my heart out one Sunday a month. For over a year I did that. It wasn't about me, and I didn't know that I had the opportunity to be embarrassed. I'm glad in retrospect that it took a kind of bravery to not be stopped by potential ridicule or judgment from myself or others.

In what way can you set aside judgment, access your own kind of bravery, and dance a little today?

108 | *A bird uses wind and air to minimize effort and support their soaring.*

In the early days of flight, the load that the plane carried was a major safety and function consideration. There are hair-raising stories of airplanes amidst storms jettisoning goods to provide maximum loft to rise above the weather event. Although capacity has increased substantially, the Federal Aviation Administration still governs maximum takeoff weight for all aircraft.

The metaphor is natural.

- The lighter the load,
- the easier the lift,
- the higher the loft.

In a world where the usual chant is some form of "Bigger, better, faster" and the business world's advice equates to, "Scale up and earn more," it's important to consider each addition to your own life's flight plan. Always ask, "Will this help me fly?"

How will this lift, or give loft? Will this help me fly? Will it support you as you soar?

Can you minimize or illuminate one thing that you know weighs you down?

109 | *Being present and accepting of the breadth of human experience takes courage.*

It's a popular phrase: Feel all the feels. Connie Bennett, retired librarian, understands there are layers to the looking. She advises, "Look for the second wave of feeling after the flood of first feelings passes."

It takes fortitude to fully experience and attempt to understand the first wave of feelings. An even greater portion of personal courage is required to look for and welcome the second wave. A strong case can be made for having the capacity to fully allow these waves. Welcoming them and learning from their natural flow keeps them from becoming a tsunami of feelings, literally an emotional weather event, stored up for some stormy release. When I was learning to surf, an old surfer gave me advice that I have summarized in memory this way: *"Take the wave that comes to you. Don't spend your day wasting ride opportunities by gambling on a better wave coming along."*

When feelings are greeted in their authentic reality, without all of the *shoulds* and *oughts*, they can be some of the finest teachers and trainers. Take the wave when it comes to you.

How can you ride all the waves of your true feelings in some way today?

110 | *Things that you don't even know you need conspire to arrive with their own ineffable timing.*

Be watchful. What can look like an interruption to a plan is often a resolution or solution you didn't know you needed.

Most narratives of a life-changing moment initially describe it as an undesirable event, even a crisis: divorce, disasters, devastating betrayals. These are utterly undesirable events measured on their own. Yet taken in the context of all that comes after, they are inexplicably instrumental in delivering key lessons, as well as a changed and often improved circumstance.

Jeanette Richardson Herring shares, *"The sweetest moments often follow the unimaginable. I don't look for the devastations to*

find what follows, but I'm quick to observe what does arrive in the
wake. It is often love."

When my landlords gave me less than thirty days' notice to
relocate, I was devastated. My plan had been to remain in that spot
for some years, and they'd said repeatedly that they hoped I would
stay since I was their ideal renter. The news created upheaval, grief,
uncertainty. This circumstance, which felt disastrous, gave rise to the
manifestation of an incredible circle of support from friends near and
far. Ultimately, it transported me across the country, to circumstances
that have improved my well-being and led me to an unimaginably
joyous living environment. Is this some sort of weird optimism at play?
No. It is not as the ancient wisdom suggests, "My barn having burned
to the ground, I can now see the moon." It is more like…"Since my
barn burned down, I can now rebuild the structure that ideally suits
its relationship to the property and meets my current needs."

In what appears to be undesirable in this day, can you
suspect some potential positive promise or outcome?

||| *Have the vulnerability and*
courage to create in community.

Politicians through the decades have been fond of saying that we
are stronger together. The truth of this may be disclosed by your
own experience. Even in those pinnacle moments of individual
accomplishment, you have to ask yourself if you really accomplished

the thing all on your own. It's more than likely there were communities that cheered you on, supported you, contributed, and stood up for you and with you along the way. It may seem that you lead alone or make decisions alone, yet even the ancestors object to that view. I vote because women marched and sacrificed their lives for my capacity to do so. I have certain rights because a community of people showed up, stood up, and spoke up.

The poet John Donne correctly observed that no one exists as an island.

In *Winnie-the-Pooh*, author A.A. Milne allows Piglet to observe that everything is better when done with two. Even as a lifelong introvert, I know this to be true.

Will you allow practical experience as a community member to impact your day?

112 | *Blessed: to be given a thing, to be endowed.*

The state of blessedness can be interpreted as a pleasure or relief in contrast to an undesirable state of being. Often people say they are blessed with returning health. In the first meaning (to be given a thing), one is a recipient. It is a gift, often gratefully received. In the second definition (to be endowed), there's a greater level of personal involvement. It manifests as appreciation or gratitude.

These two definitions form a powerful partnership. By embracing a clear gratefulness for what has been bestowed, one experiences a sense of great fortune. Recognizing that not all graces are either earned or deserved but are rather given magnanimously, even objectively, allows a deeper sense of blessedness to surface.

How can you increase your awareness today of your blessedness?

113 | *Friendship is a stepping-stone on almost every path toward a goal.*

Every once in a while, as a way of checking in with myself, I try to think of an accomplishment, a milestone, or a completed goal that I have achieved entirely on my own. I can never think of even one thing. This inquiry reinforces the appreciation and gratitude I have for my friends and my family. With very few exceptions, a friend or many friends have paved the way for me on virtually every fine path I followed and every road long traveled. In spite of the do-it-yourself and go-it-alone mentality that permeates layers of society, most elements of my life either exist because of or have been improved by the community in which I circle.

Is today a good day to acknowledge or thank a friend for the way they have contributed to your life?

Love is a great beginning to an experience and it is a tender ending.

Liz Amaya-Fernandez, doula, educator, and poet, calls all motivation into question in the context of love. She asks, "If not for love, then why?"

It may be tempting to ask: How does love apply to a corporate endeavor? Love applies like medicine; like a balm, a Band-Aid, or water. Love applies like wide blue sky. Love applies by asking what might go right, by listening, by waiting, by knowing that someone may be doing their best.

Just asking the question helps apply love. If love isn't involved, why exactly are you involved?

In a world that significantly values hard skills, with an emphasis on productivity and profitability, it has become easy for some to skirt this motivation entirely. Can love fit on a spreadsheet? Can love be measured as an element of a production sequence? It may require following a circling and winding thread...but love, or the absence of love, hovers under or near most actions. Even actions that seem to rise from obligation can track back to love or a love once held. Why would you do anything if not ultimately for love?

People before projects: Some days start with a profoundly packed list of projects. And then there are unexpected beloveds who show up for help, for fun, for a listen. I whisper to my production manager's daughter-self, "People before projects." It can be tempting at the end of some days to express in exasperation, "I didn't get a single thing on my list done." Perhaps I forgot at the start of the day to put love on the list.

Will you follow your threads and find answers specific to you regarding how love applies?

115 | *Be generous with your praise. Reward the behavior you want to see again.*

Good boy. *Good* boy. What a good dog you are. Webster doesn't always need a treat as incentive for good behavior. Enthusiastic words of praise feed his good-dog soul. This is true for human creatures as well.

People may say they do not require praise. Yet even plants thrive when kind words and praises are delivered to them on a consistent basis. Psychologists support this premise, generally believing that praise reinforces a sense of self-worth. Praise has to be genuine and merited in order for the positive impact to happen. Insincere praise can be demotivating.

Will you listen for times you are praised today and look for opportunities to praise others?

Questions don't always have immediate answers; they point toward the path of an answer.

I spoke to a Rotary club when I was a teenager. They recited what they called The Four-Way Test. It made a lifelong impression on me.

1. Is it the *Truth*?
2. Is it *Fair* to all concerned?
3. Will it build *Goodwill* and better *Friendships*?
4. Will it be *Beneficial* to all concerned?

Two decades later, I recognized my team needed a metric by which they could measure their customer service responses. I created what became our Three-Way Test. The metrics of value, quality, and intention continue to influence me to this day.

Radmacher's Three-Way Test:

- Increase: Does it add *Value*?
- Improve: Does it improve *Quality*?
- Impact: Does it have consequences for my *Intentions*?

If you developed a metric or test by which you evaluated all of your exchanges, what might that be?

Connect to promise. Connect to premise. Connect to people.

The American people have moved closer to isolation both in certain aspects of political drive and some social structures. The many issues individuals face can either muddy priorities or bring what matters into sharp focus. Studies have proved for decades that connection is essential for an infant to have a better chance of healthy, stable, and positive relationships as an adult. Connecting to others is not a matter of choice for an infant, but it *is* a matter of choice for an adult.

Consciously connecting with others is also key for adults to have positive relationships. This choice is manifested in many ways: kindness with strangers and intentional, authentic grace with friends and beloveds. To intentionally connect requires attentive energy and mindfulness. It is an investment that can deliver fabulous interest. Or the actual return on investment may occur in the singular action of making the thoughtful choice to connect.

How will you identify opportunities to increase your connections?

The underbrush is the coolest spot in a hot day.

My friends are a cooling wind,

my learnings are a bed made with line-dried cotton sheets

my making of things is the constancy of a gentle evening
breeze cooling off a hot summer day,

my words shelter in my soul, temper any hurricane in spirit,
and assuage any fevered heat,

the windows rolled down on a well-traveled road allow
the breeze of cool speed clarity to blow through my hair
and vehicle.

My cool spot is found in the cultivated garden of what
matters most.

Reflecting on this idea, Jean Robin Martell shares, *"My cool spot
is in a flower garden where I bask in their fragrances and colors.
Being among the trees refreshes me with cool breezes. The sky and
clouds call to me, and my mood lifts just looking up. Sometimes the
clouds open and shower the earth with cleansing water. Another
cooling off period. Lakes, rivers, and oceans have the power to cleanse
and cool as well. My cool spots exist in nature. As I cross the many
thresholds I find in the natural world, I move from one spot to the
next, one joy to another."*

Do you know where your cool spot is and might you use
it today?

I come to the sea to breathe.

Where do I breathe most easily and deeply? Is that included in this
plan, effort, choice?

I have decades of evidence that I thrive in a different sort of
way when I am near the sea. Absent an ocean, I do well to be near
any kind of water. When considering a creative sabbatical, I always
evaluate proximity to water when determining the location. Knowing
that space/place/spot where I can easily be at ease is a component of
my successful experiences.

A kindness that is often overlooked is that of our own attentiveness
to the ways and places in which we thrive.

Where is your spot where you breathe most readily? How long
since you've been there? If you cannot travel there now or are not
currently located there, can you benefit from closing your eyes and
imagining yourself in that place?

**How might your day be different if you kindly included
spaces and places that contribute to your wellness
and effectiveness?**

Can I be a mirror of kindness in this?

A mirror of kindness would reflect back to the source: A kindness extended is a kindness returned. This is the epitome of reciprocity. In the language of metaphor, what if your mirror holds the reflection of kindness and allows you to carry it forward? What if it allows you to hold that kindness as a container would hold it, for a short period of time? It would be held for a time when that kindness is required by someone else or needed for your own self. This is the crux of the directive, "pay it forward." With reciprocity *and* regeneration, it is possible to both reflect kindness and carry kindness ahead, to take action toward the good, toward kindness, creating a benefit or advantage to someone or something.

In the face of what appears to be a great unsolvable condition, it is tempting to become paralyzed by the enormity of the need. To remain inert in the face of large problems or even enormous opportunity can be seized as a necessary pause. Leverage your motionless moments to consider your role. Recognize you may not be able to dismantle an entire ancient wall. What you *can* do is remove a few of the stones and place them where they can realize a greater good. Your actions need not bear the weight of solving the whole of a thing, it can be a single step, a single kind action toward the good.

Manifesting and acting on these functions allow you to be a magic mirror of kindness.

How will you allow kindness to be reflected in your choices and actions?

|2| Appreciate the open hand of a friend.

At first glance, it may appear odd to associate courage with the capacity to receive, to accept the open hand of help from a friend. It's complicated, as they say. And it is also simple. We are taught that it is better to give than receive. It sounds noble on the surface, doesn't it? And it is so comforting a thought because it is incredibly familiar, having been repeated in so many different ways over the years. However, there is a different, somewhat insidious element to this ubiquitous trope. Replace the word "better" with the two-word phrase, "more powerful."

To be the chronic giver and resistant receiver is a position near the top in the power hierarchy. It becomes an impenetrable place that is exceptionally one-sided. Samuel Clemens, writing as Mark Twain, addressed the conundrum that occurs when giving and receiving is a one-sided equation, when a human only gives and never receives. He wrote, "If you pick up a starving dog and make him prosperous, he will not bite you. This is a principal difference between a dog and a man." Always giving or always receiving creates an imbalance that is ultimately reflected in behavior.

Being in a position of continual receiving produces an element of resentment. Being in a position of continually giving and never receiving produces a condition of dominance. Reciprocity is an equalizer. It is the thing that promotes give and take. Promotion of self-determinism as a life practice has driven individuals to want to take 100 percent credit for their own success. It becomes culturally difficult to acknowledge all the contributions that others have made along the way. There really is no such thing as a self-made person.

Vulnerability requires courage. The most happy, successful people are those who are vulnerable enough to accept help, and who appreciate the assistance and acknowledge the open hands of their friends.

Can you call to mind the picture of an open hand and be ready to release and receive?

122 | *There are great memories, joys, and friendships to be cultivated in the context of community.*

The Irish word for community is *pobal*. It's pronounced pub-ell. The bars in Ireland are called pubs and it's tempting to claim the name is rooted in their word for community! It's actually a shortened term from the centuries old reference to a "public house." It really is a neighborhood's living room. In the primary room of a modern pub, there will be a broad cross-section of the population, including children. In older times (and as recently as a 1993 in rural western Ireland), women were relegated to a different room. Pubs in Ireland have largely left that custom behind. Much of a community's news, art, and culture may be found centered in a local pub. The spirit of community and welcome, or "Fáilte," is manifested as a model in an Irish pub.

Leanore Curran shares a familial memory associated with the pub culture. *"My father, from Glasgow, Scotland, visited our neighborhood 'pub' daily (after retiring) at 3:00 p.m. on the dot. Same people, same servers, same community. When he got ill, he would still walk to and from with his oxygen tank. We had a small wake at this pub, after his funeral. The place was packed. I looked at 'his' empty chair. No one sat on that chair for weeks. There was all sorts of laughing and storytelling. And plenty of 'the water of life' (whiskey) shared between friends who missed the center of this pub and his wicked sense of humor."*

Heather Mack, a collaborative minister, observes, *"Community can be messy, silly, infuriating…but in real communities, there is always room for one more person, one more story, and one more hug."*

Digital connectivity has dramatically impacted the definition of community. In decades past, it was localized. People communicated over distance with postal correspondence, via telegram, and later, with telephone calls. But such connection came with a cost. Most community contexts were physical and local. Now, with the Internet and various social platforms, there is vital and dynamic community formed all around the world, not tied to a single physical location. Regardless of technological advances, community of any sort is cultivated by hospitality, genuinely welcoming inclusivity, and relationship.

What can you do to show up for a dose of community conviviality today?

123 | *Kindness does not have a place on a map, it is the map.*

I ask myself often to attribute the quality of compassion or kindness to a familiar physical object. It helps me identify and stay connected to the opportunities for generosity at a particular moment. Perhaps you've seen the water features at Disney World or something like them. Picture a large, calm lake, mirroring a bold blue sky, serene, its water undisturbed. Then? You catch the sound of a rumble, small at first, but rising in volume. With unanticipated force, a tower of water shoots straight up out of the previously tranquil lagoon. Then, dozens of other water streams begin their journey up and cascading down. All kinds of fountains spring forth.

You are the lake, and the fountain action is your spontaneous kindness. In the natural world, this is called a geyser, where the hot springs erupt, bubbling upward from deep in the crest of the earth. In a man-made context, it springs forth with extraordinary momentum manufactured to reflect the phenomenon first seen in the natural world. This man-made creation is brought about by a plan. An actual geyser is controlled by physical conditions well beyond the control of humankind. In either event, as an observer, you have no capacity to intervene or change when the fountain is going to spring forth. It bubbles up of its own accord. Like a natural impulse toward goodness, it is the thing that rises up unexpectedly and washes over you.

It's tempting to second-guess the impulse toward kindness. You might worry about how it will be received, or if it is enough, or too much. It's a generally accepted metric that erring on the side of kindness is rarely a mistake. An ancient understanding, Proverbs 16:24, compares a kind word to a honeycomb, suggesting it is a sweetness to the soul.

Delivering undesirable news is a difficult and oft required task. Communicating clearly and delivering the harsh reality with a bit of kindness makes it more bearable. Perhaps kindness can be understood as a softening of what otherwise would be unyielding; a gentling of a thing—not essential to a core equation, and yet by bringing it into the calculation, the resulting computation comes more effortlessly. Kindness can loosen a grip, release a knot, or quicken a resolution.

Where is it possible to leave space in your day for kindness to spring up?

Each time a chance for a studied look springs up, something new is seen.

Spring as a noun is a season. Spring as a verb is in the first definition an action—to actually spring into action, leap, jump, bound! As a noun and a verb, they share some qualities. But the definition that captivates my attention is the secondary meaning of the verb "to spring;" one less frequently used, it is a reference to origin. It means to originate or arise from.

The world is full of apparent contradictions. It is populated by things that appear as opposites, yet are actually on either end of a continuum. As the old adage suggests, they are "two sides of the same coin."

Apples and oranges—the experience of them is so different. One is solid, crisp, sweet, resistant to the teeth; the other made up of defined sections, tart, easily pierced by the teeth. Both are members of the fruit family, both originate as tree fruit. Cats, dogs—their chromosome pairs differ in quantity, yet both spring from the group of quadrupedal animals.

That fight you had, again, with that one particular human that is so very different than you? You spring from the same genetic sequence as that human. Drilling down in the layers of differences often finds that a commonality springs forth.

This applies to types of decisions and elements of skills, talents, and abilities. That second and third look will often reveal that these things which appear so divergent actually spring from the same source. "Look, again, always look again."

How can looking anew at something frequently observed generate a positive result?

125 | *Be like water.*

When one pauses to consider all the different things water does, it makes the phrase "water is life" make absolute sense. In the contemplation of all the ways water works, consider the body. There, water allows for digestion and converts food into fuel, provides essentials for cells to operate and replicate, processes waste, paves the brain's pathways, regulates body temperature, oxygenates the body, and makes up more than 60 percent of the body's mass. In ways parallel to the human body, water is essential to life on the planet.

Access to clean water becomes a political and cultural metric of equality. Refusing access to clean water is a weapon that the powerful use against the vulnerable. Often the cost of oil and gas are discussed; they are reported regularly by news outlets. There is a gas gauge available to measure how much fuel is required to make a vehicle run. We are less conscious of how much water is essential for the optimal operation of a body, or our planet. The availability of clean water is more frequently considered when it is not available. People chronically exposed to water scarcity, or regions subject to drought, understand this in ways that modern urban dwellers do not. There are those times with electric grid outages or frozen pipes, when citizens are reminded of the pervasive role that water plays in every element of life.

To "be like water" is an overwhelming directive. It is said that a rising tide lifts all boats. This reflects the equity that exists when everyone has access to clean, abundantly supplied water. In the phrase "be like water," you are asked to help and support all systems, your own and those around you, to be nourished and work even more efficiently.

Will you notice the systems that you support and that support you that may be like water?

126 | *Have a long memory for joy and a short memory for disappointment.*

I left the grocery store. The item on the top of my list was out of stock. I was disappointed; it was the focus of my dinner plan, and I was really looking forward to it. The disappointment lasted just minutes. I remember it now because it happened recently. It seems unlikely I'll remember it even in a week, although the item was buttermilk for biscuits, so it might take a week and a half!

In 1983, I applied for a job at a manufacturing plant in the human resources department. It was a step down from the executive position I had just left in San Francisco. I was young, I'd just returned to my hometown, and I needed a job. I knew it was a good fit and would provide me lots of different learning opportunities. I was confident the job was mine—until the moment it wasn't. When I was called with the news, I did what all unsuccessful candidates are supposed to do. Graciously, I asked if I could have done anything differently to have had a different result. The head of the department said I was actually the best candidate but that company policy favors applicants with degrees. I had all the qualifications she wanted but not that one. In the quiet of my apartment, I replayed all of the life events that had deferred the education I had planned on. The disappointment was palpable. To this day, I can see the place I was standing when I received the news. The memory is long, perhaps because it is paired with a contrasting experience. Three days later, I received a second call. The successful applicant had declined the job offer, and would I accept the position? Yes.

I can't easily recall hosts of other single disappointments with such vivid detail because they simply have not remained in my memory. The memories of disappointment that are indelible are the ones that stand in a line and become something larger than the single pivot point. I contextualize the conglomerations of certain disappointing life events as lessons, as notable patterns, and continue to learn from them.

Independent and single joyful events do remain in my memory—happily and long. It is said that what one focuses on enlarges. This makes me grateful that on the whole, I give safe heart-harbor to the experiences of joy.

What do you allow to dwell long in your memory?

The moments of our lives are a rare commodity with an unknown span.

Some years after my last visit to Paris, I reflected on my changed plans. It was spring. I planned to return to Paris for an even longer stay that same year, in the autumn. Things changed in my life, and the change was substantial. I did not return to the city of lights, La Ville-Lumière, much to my disappointment. Although I cross the bridges, shop the stamp market, and walk the boulevards often in my imagination, I have yet to return. Perhaps I never will.

Of this I wrote, "If I had known I would not return to Paris, I would have lingered over my coffee a little longer."

I only know one legitimate answer to the question that Elizabeth Crouch often asks herself, "How much time do I have, really?" That answer is: this. This moment, this right now. The much-celebrated practice of envisioning, intending, planning our future is an interesting companion to living in the now. It's a functional contradiction and one that I find unnecessary to try and reconcile.

Dr. Martina McGowan, poet, summarizes, *"We often forget that this is all we have for certain. We need the reminder to relish this and every other moment while we are in it."*

Sharon Martinelli told me that one of her favorite spiritual leaders, while at a retreat, gave her the phrase, *"Linger a moment longer."* When she recalls that phrase, it slows her down and allows her to be fully present to the moment.

However you choose to remind yourself of the precious nature of our moments, will you remember throughout the day?

128 | *Allow your own best interests to be included in any planning or significant considerations.*

It's tempting for some people to place their own best interests at the bottom of any list. You can see this reflected in an ordinary experience: a host may announce to the many gathered guests that food for the occasion is now available on the buffet table. Yet in spite of the general invitation, no one wants to go first. Taking the first place in line is somehow equated to taking the last cookie on the plate; no one is inclined to do it.

It takes an element of chutzpah—of nerve—to stand up and be willing to be first in line, first to answer, or the first to accept something that is being offered. We are schooled by modes of civility and a concern regarding what other people will think. Some folks are deeply interested in how they appear to others, and they don't want to look selfish or overly self-interested.

There are many times in life when an individual is called upon to consider their own best interests as at least as important as someone else's. In some instances, considering your own best interest before that of others is advisable, even required. It's now a common advisory–one that you'll hear with every set of safety instructions delivered on an in airplane in the US as well as many other countries: "In the unlikely event that oxygen will be required, secure your own mask before assisting others with theirs."

This practical instruction crosses age, experience, and enterprise. If your own interests and capacity are not at a well-tended level, you are not able to tend to the best interests of others. There comes a time when you must overlook the impression you are making on others and have the courage to make decisions on behalf of your own best interests and practices. When the host invites guests to come to the table, if you are hungry? Go first! It provides the beneficial service of leading the way, making it easier for others to fall in line behind you.

In what ways do you make certain that your best interests are being addressed?

129 | *Giving and receiving equally well are partners in a courageous life.*

Part of being an excellent giver is the capacity to graciously receive. One-sided generosity overlooks an important relationship element: reciprocity. The capacity to accept is just as significant as the capacity to give. Chronic giving without any reciprocal receiving is fertile soil for planting martyrdom, bitterness, resentment, and all manner of dysfunctional attributes. Chronic receiving without accompanying giving misses one of the finest opportunities of being human: generosity of spirit.

The Latin term *quid pro quo* implies the required exchange of equal value, meaning literally, "what for what." A common translation of this is "tit for tat." That phrase emerged from the words tip and tap, which reflect a hit or a light blow. It's come to mean, in a very negative context, returning an insult with equal force—which typically escalates any conflict.

Giving is not a competition. Receiving is a grace. You know people who resist accepting a compliment and will argue regarding their worthiness of the assessment. To simply say thank you is a grace. To give without expectation of return is a grace. To receive without obligation to resist or match the gift is also a grace. There are many ways to be reciprocal. In the practice of both giving and receiving with graciousness, the quickest default response is, "Thank you."

Watch how you receive what is given.

130 | *In the kind heart, there is always an opportunity for generous service.*

The opportunity for service and/or generosity is available in every twist and turn of our journey. Service isn't always obvious, and generosity has a larger capacity than is conventionally held. Acting in service can mean listening to a contradictory opinion, asking considered questions, and getting a better understanding of the other view. This is both in service to the other by deepening their grasp on their own view and service to self in developing a broader perspective. Contrary to the impulse to define both service and generosity as doing and giving a tangible thing, remaining silent can be a service as well. Being present simply as a witness is a generosity of spirit. Taking action or giving money are basic and immediate impulses.

"What are the opportunities for service and/or generosity in this instance? Is one of them mine to do?"

Leanore Curran recounts, *"Years ago, the idea of saying no didn't appeal to me because I was deathly afraid I would hurt feelings. Thanks to time, wisdom, and thoughtful friends, I'm finally able to guide myself to making better choices—for myself. I described being overly busy as 'productivity,' and gauged my entire reputation on how much I could do in any given day. Thank you for this wonderful and beautiful opportunity to think about life and how our days unfold. I jumped off the treadmill of life and am finally taking time to ponder decisions and what is best suited for me."*

Ironically, the most significant service can be not being in service. Occasionally, the highest generosity is allowing your *no* to become someone else's *yes*. An internal whisper in your ear while exploring this question might be, "Is this my right opportunity, or does it belong to someone else? Just because you can doesn't mean you ought."

Noticing an opportunity doesn't automatically make it your opportunity. Being able to be generous is not the same as knowing it is correct for you to give.

How might it impact your experience if you evaluate whether an opportunity truly belongs to you?

Kindness must be understood apart from being nice.

It's stayed with me for decades. C.S. Lewis and his first Narnia Chronicle, *The Lion, The Witch, and The Wardrobe*, has the anxious Susan asking Mr. Beaver about the safety involved in meeting a lion. His answer has dramatically influenced me. "Safe? Who said anything about safe? 'Course he isn't safe. But he's good."

A similar conversation has been an internal dialogue for decades. It covers the difference between being nice and being kind and the distance between the two. The explanation is often heard, particularly in arguments, "I was just being nice." Rarely do you hear someone defending an attitude, statement, or action with the qualifier (which is dismissive), "I was just being kind." Nice implies an element of deception, of the not-quite-true and disingenuous. Kind is authentic, dependably trustworthy. Girlfriends know the difference between these two things experientially. Being nice is exemplified in this: "Does this bright red color look good on me?" The answer? "Yes."

Being kind looks and sounds like this: "Does this color look good on me?" The response, "I believe jewel-tone cobalt is your better color. This red is not a favorite for you."

Truth can have a hard smack. Kindness discerns the way to be direct, to honestly respond, without also being harsh. Nice is convenient. Nice concerns itself with appearances. Kindness is sometimes inconvenient. It requires considered evaluation and thoughtful response; it involves compassion and a level of empathy.

Kindness is a key component of mercy. Actually, kindness does indeed have an element of mercy in it—it is extended without measure of merit. That's the mercy part. Kindness is often offered as a defining characteristic of the giver, not really anything about the recipient. Genuine kindness is not earned, it is unqualified. Kindness is an element in some social contracts, and it is not limited to humans. Webster, my canine pal, demonstrates a keen kindness. In fact, humanity can take lessons on kindness from much of the animal kingdom. All around us there are master classes in kindness.

Am I nice? Absolutely not. I might not be particularly safe or even good, either. However, I am kind. What are some significant roles that kindness plays?

- Shifts perspective
- Overshadows annoyance
- Calms fear of deficit or lack
- Softens the edges of grief
- Acts as a lifeline toward hope
- Makes goodness even sweeter
- Creates a bridge in the midst of disharmony
- Improves relationships, when gratitude is experienced and expressed
- Is an element in physical well-being, as gratitude is an element of emotional well-being
- Often determines or informs directions and decisions

- Sparks more kind actions when previous kindnesses are recounted (as well as quality sleep, particularly if done right before bedtime)

I have applied Kathleen Everett's oft-referenced metric, "Reward that behavior you want to see more of" broadly to myself, my friends, and even my dogs! In much the same way that Marie Kondo insists that for things to remain in your environment they must evoke joy, I know that when I populate my calendar, promises, courses, and interactions with people and things that articulate kindness, I feel abundant. A sense of mutuality or reciprocity rises up out of my keen awareness of received and extended kindnesses. This is not a circumstance of quid pro quo (I'll do *this* because you did *that*), but rather actions that bubble up over the top of a container that is full of grace. Oregon Health Sciences University Hospital saved my life when I was not yet two years old. Since comprehending their role in the fact that I am still alive, my appreciation has led me to contribute to organizations that save children's lives. Kindness consistently informs decisions about giving. A commitment to kindness determines direction and promotes memorable decisions.

What role could kindness play in the decisions of the day?

*Courage manages
to speak up for
itself and others,
even when the voice
is barely a whisper
and even when it
has to repeat itself.*

| # How will I tend my own fire to keep it burning?

One person knows better than anyone what it takes to keep your energy on an even keel…to keep your internal fire burning evenly and long. That one person is you.

- How will you fuel yourself to meet the physical demands ahead of you?
- How will you invest in your own growth and learning?
- How will you sustain a level of joy, or at least enjoyment, in the many tasks and actions required of you?

Others may have ideas, and yet you are the only one who knows what keeps your own flame burning brightly. After you identify, with specificity, what those things are, make a practical plan for sustaining them.

In the movie *The Princess Bride*, the evil chancellor Tyrone tells the king, "Get some rest. If you haven't got your health, you haven't got anything." Countless versions of that advice exist in literature and real life. It's repeated often because it is so very true. Operating from a place of wellness and health provides the most optimal pivot point for embracing opportunity and change. For those in a space of physical challenge, reaching toward a broader level of health is the practice. In the face of the great need of another, it is tempting for a caregiver to overlook their own needs and disregard signs of their own unwellness. Our culture applauds this kind of sacrifice. I immediately return to that phrase beginning, "if you haven't got your health."

When I prioritize my own health, I am more capable of supporting the needs and health of others.

How can you tend your own health first, consistently and dynamically?

133 | *Be the gardener of your own field.*

When wild flower seed is scattered over soil, scattered is the operative word. I received a package of wildflower seed as a gift. It was such a good experience. I enjoyed randomly tossing the seeds in the field that met my backyard. It was a pleasure to watch them as they variously popped up all over the place.

Purposely acquired or saved seeds or bulbs are usually treated differently. They are part of a larger gardening plan. They require specific types of shade or sun to grow at their optimal level. These seeds or bulbs are sewn with a purpose and special care because they each have a specific place where they best belong—an ideal place.

This is an ideal lesson from the natural world for many things, like the time you expend and the products or services that you make, craft, and offer. Perhaps it applies to almost any kind of offer or service. Knowing what need a specific thing fills helps you know how to talk about it. Knowing the niche your product occupies informs you of the audience it requires. Being familiar with the scope of your service makes certain that you are tending it appropriately.

As you consider your activities today, are you certain they belong in your field?

134 | *Am I following my dream or someone else's dream?*

The ancestors. My ancestors. Perhaps they had dreams for an as yet unborn girl-child. I cannot know. I have known very few of them. Dreams for the future were not a specific point of conversation in my immediate family except for discussion of the ones that were not possible. The best support for dreaming my mother offered was leaving the door open to the outdoors and not keeping me inside. Often left to my own devices, I learned how it felt to pursue an action that had personal meaning and curiosity attached to it.

My father did not craft the activity in the context of a dream when he opened the latest *Readers Digest* to the "increase your word power" section. Did he know he was fostering a dream of pursuing meaningful word crafting throughout my entire life? I cannot know. It was never topical. And yet, the monthly exercise of it nurtured a deeply held dream. My older sister made it possible for me to have dreams of any sort. As a nursing student home on break, she intervened in my medical crisis as a not-yet-two-year-old. Her keen assessment and quick actions saved my life. My other sister made sure I fell in love with books. It was a straight, short walk to the local library branch, and before I was even six, she provided opportunities to open thousands of dreams held behind seemingly ordinary spines on shelf after shelf. In this way, she did not insist that I follow a certain dream. She made sure I had access to the knowledge that supports a dream. This access was accompanied by an adult library card long before my age qualified me for one. In retrospect, I see that while they did not conversationally promote the idea of identifying and pursuing a dream, they experientially promoted actions that made it possible for me to recognize how to follow a dream—my own dream, not theirs.

Dreams imposed by others masquerade as many things: obligation, expectation, familial or societal norms. Pursuing a dream that has the complete dedication of my whole heart conjures up the image of a ship in full sail; a boat with great momentum, propelled forward by the smallest wind because of the full set of the sail. When the sail is not set, it doesn't matter what wind there is—it simply flops about. Untrained, unset, the sail is useless, unable to realize the task that it was crafted to fulfill. This is apt metaphor for what it is to live someone else's dream. Simply because you are qualified or gifted to do a thing does not mean it is yours to do. I was instructed in 1974, after completing an extensive battery of evaluative tests for a career counselor, that with my exceptional hand-eye coordination, I could go on to get a job pulling out burnt potato chips at the Frito-Lay factory. (Those verbal and written skills which ranked in the top percentile was not a matter of consideration for career guidance with that individual at that time.) Turns out that hand-eye coordination skill ultimately served my dream of creating beautiful handmade cards in my own original art production company. My dream, followed, has led me here, to you, this very day. Full sail. Forward momentum still.

What is your answer to the question, "Does this dream really belong to me?"

|35 | *Punctuate movement with stillness.*

Our movement and activity driven culture emphasizes that you should surround yourself with movement. Go. Get. Do. Count those steps. Go to the gym. Scale that wall. Jump. Sit in meetings. Document things. Swim. Run. Shop here. Dine out. Travel. Go there, and then? still go go go go go!

The demand for and insistence upon movement overwhelms the quiet invitation of stillness.

It surprises some to learn that what many of the world's wealthiest and most "successful" people prize most is their time spent in stillness; quiet moments given over to thinking and reflection. The world calls these people "the movers and shakers." However, in narrative and in interviews, these individuals affirm that they are able to move the mountains that they do by first punctuating their movement and their shaking with stillness and with solid thinking.

Do you have the confidence to sit still with your thoughts?

Am I vulnerable in an undesirable way?

It happens every time before I step on stage. Whether I am delivering a keynote or playing a role in a performance, I get nervous. My breathing quickens; my heart rate increases. This is evidence of a good kind of vulnerability. I am willing to authentically put myself in a circumstance of exposure.

Undesirable vulnerability shares many of those same physical attributes, plus an undeniable anxiety.

When I wrote the phrase "Walk to the edge" in the "Live With Intention" poem, I was remembering the time I was at the edge of the sheer drop of the Cliffs of Moher in Ireland. It was a tip-off of things to come in my primary relationship with the person at my side. That individual was often careless of me and not always accidentally. No fence, no restraint at this edge, and one swift thoughtless move would've sent me to my death. I moved away from his reach. I felt vulnerable in an undesirable way.

Am I vulnerable in the best possible way?

Webster loved the dog park in our new town. It was well-maintained, the people were friendly, and Webster thrived chasing the ball. As a stranger in a new state, it was comforting to arrive daily to the dog park and have people call out Webster's name and my own.

It was New Year's Eve, and this friendly, energetic rat terrier I keep company with was resting between ball chases. A woman I did not recognize arrived with a dog I'd never seen. In less than sixty seconds, her dog was after Webster. All of Webster's four-legged friends rushed away as this newcomer lunged at Webster. My little fella tried to get away but could not outmaneuver the attacking animal. The dog's owner was pulling at its tail in an attempt to get him off Webster. The effort was unsuccessful. Then Webster did something that utterly surprised me. He rolled on his back, utterly exposed his belly, and tucked his head into his chest. Later, hours later, when I had stopped the bleeding and found a dog hospital open on New Year's Eve, I was told by the vet that Webster's purposeful position of vulnerability saved his life. His throat had been pierced, yes, but it was not in the worst spot. He gave the aggressor a larger field to attack by exposing his belly, and he protected the most vulnerable portion of his neck by bending it to his torso. He also transmitted a message that most dogs, even aggressive ones, understand. By this position of exposure, Webster was telling the attacking dog, "I am no threat to you." That moment of vulnerability gave the owner the chance to pull her dog away. With instinct and animal wisdom, Webster made himself vulnerable in the best possible way given these undesirable circumstances.

As you consider that this intentional vulnerability saved my dog's life, can you ask yourself when and how you might choose to be more vulnerable?

How does your body recognize the reality of a vulnerable circumstance? In what way can you listen and be aware of exposure to an undesirable vulnerability?

137 *What peer group can review this with informed eyes?*

Authors understand the value of objective readers putting their attention on a manuscript. Asking friends to review a project is often comforting and supportive, but not necessarily likely to provide the candid assessment that will serve the work most effectively.

Your project can benefit with review from informed eyes. A group with expertise in the focus of endeavor or industry can offer a particular sort of evaluation. Allowing consideration by people completely unfamiliar with the process, and even unfamiliar with you, can yield surprising results. Invite informed eyes trained in unrelated disciplines to review your endeavor. This particular consideration often generates a surprisingly innovative analysis.

Would something of yours benefit from review today? Ask informed eyes and be resolved to consider the review.

138 *Enough is enough.*

Enough. It is a sign of confidence to know when the level of enough has been reached:
- Enough tolerating unacceptable behavior
- Enough food in your pantry
- Enough money in your bank account
- Enough in reserve for retirement or emergencies

- Enough food on your plate
- Enough commitments on your agenda
- Enough meaningful activity
- Enough love in your heart

Sue Robson likes to *"remember to create 'Yay lists.' To review what I was able to do, create, overcome, and even shifts of perception. In reviewing, I remind myself of the growth and good I am experiencing, and ultimately, I become more confident and trusting of myself."*

It's no mystery that most conscientious humans are their own worst critics. There's a temptation to identify all the ways more could have been done. I have a friend whose process always includes identifying every way they can think of to improve what they just did or made. It's their consistent one-person debriefing. I have been assured that this is their way of being a lifelong learner and that it is not self-criticism—even though it may sound like it! This is an exception to the lack of affirmation and positive self-talk that most people provide themselves.

Another friend was being critical of her own activities and asserted, "I haven't done anything for at least six weeks." What was more accurate would have gone, *"My personal and specific identified priorities have been usurped by unexpected personal issues and multiple needs of others."* I went ahead and made a list for her to demonstrate that she had experienced six weeks of nonstop service to the needs and priorities of others. It was a pretty large list.

Will you find a way to affirm and validate all that you accomplish in and offer to this day, including even the unplanned for things?

139 | *Willingness is the finest companion to your unconventional vision.*

This includes even reluctant willingness or only becoming willing after being hauled kicking and screaming toward your big, unconventional vision.

Willingness is a moment when a courageous *yes* emerges from you. Sometimes the positive inclination is expressed in a whisper. At other moments, the will and wish conspire in readiness with a rousing hoot, holler, and shout. However it sounds, willingness is companion to extraordinary adventures and unexpected innovation. It often sounds like a simple phrase, "I wonder what *this* would do... Let's see."

Kim Jayhan Pique shared, *"I've been feeling overwhelmed lately (selling a property), and I shut down my creative outlets. Just yesterday I thought, 'What if I set aside thirty minutes a day for centering?' I did that and felt nourished and refreshed. But it started with willingness. The thoughtful magic of these reminders keeps feeding my soul."*

What will your applied willingness feed today?

140 | *Can I see reward, benefit, or positive outcome?*

We can often see the reward, the trick is identifying a variety of ways to get to it! Do you ever stop to celebrate that arriving at your reward is a heroic journey?

Joseph Campbell served us well by identifying the components of navigating one's way to a positive outcome in his description of the Hero's Journey. I summarize my view of that journey:

- Everyday life
- The call comes
- Crosses threshold (the first of many)
- Faces difficulties and finds friends, including individuals who may at first appear to be enemies
- Receives guidance
- Enters the dragon's lair
- Encounters doubt and despair
- Completes the journey

I smile when I say that it could end with the familiar phrase, "lather/rinse/repeat."

Will you place yourself on a heroic journey in the course of this day?

141 | *When you connect the dots between all the things you know, you discover what you still get to learn.*

She said to her friend, "I don't know how to do that." Her friend said, "Here's how I learned how to do it."

Knowledge is generously and easily shared between friends. A friend has already gone a few steps ahead and can open a single door for a friend to pass through. There is one thing you can always know to do: Ask a friend! That asking and response connects you to all sorts of other things that you already know and informs you of other things you have yet to consider.

Once you identify the known, it is much easier to recognize the unknown or the things that you have yet to learn.

In what way can you support your own style of learning today? Can you ask a friend?

142 | *Does this ignite my enthusiasm?*

Enthusiasm: the word emerged in the middle of the sixteenth century to describe what was happening in much of the world. People were being taken up with an extraordinary fervor for God and particular religious structures and practices. In its early use, it was somewhat derogatory; in some applications, it remains derogatory today.

Masterful certified calligraphers said of me in my early career, "She is certainly enthusiastic about her lettering." It was not really offered as a compliment. I was not trained in classic calligraphic form, and I was largely ostracized from the international lettering community. In those patronizing tones, I was assessed as, at the least, enthusiastic.

With Greek and Latin roots, this word emerges from the synthesis of inspiration and God. And the roots of inspire, both Latin and Greek, are "to breathe in." To be enthused, then, is to breathe in spirit/God.

In the most positive application, enthusiasm breathes in the very thing that activates and engages with the holy thing. How do I say it? Perhaps you've heard me say it so many times and you already know... Remember and do what matters. That's where enthusiasm emerges from.

On what and how will you sprinkle enthusiasm today?

143 | *Accept that the only job that you must do today is your own.*

You've likely heard or read the quip, "Not my circus, not my monkeys." This is a mantra I repeat to myself often. Another helpful phrase I use is, "Just because you can doesn't mean you should."

People who have many different skill sets face tough choices. Another truism is, "If you want something done quickly and well, ask a busy person." You know someone like that, or you are that someone.

Yes! To do many things creates a continual swirl of meaningful tasks and activities. The emotionally rewarding assessment, often punctuated with admiration and awe, comes, "You are a force of nature! How do you manage to do it all?"

Juggling diverse tasks is a remarkable skill. When you pull in a task that someone else was supposed to complete and has not or did not, you keep a house of cards from toppling, at least for one more day. That action—that *kind* of juggling act—is unsustainable at so many levels. One result is that you teach others that it's OK to not do what they promised because you'll pick up their slack. It can become an unfortunate habit for both parties.

Watch, be mindful today: Are you focused on completing your own promises, or are you completing someone else's?

144 | *Honor your own priorities and promises.*

The most important promises are the ones we make to ourselves.

In honoring our own priorities and promises, we model to those around us how we would like to be treated.

What important promise to yourself will you honor today?

45 | *Can you recognize a repetitive pattern here?*

Looking for repetitive patterns is a profound tool. The search requires a level of diligence and tenacity. Have you ever asked yourself the question, "Why do I keep making the same mistake?" Finding the common patterns will assist you in discovering an answer. When I addressed a fresh cohort of new runners and walkers, I demonstrated the advantage of keeping an activity log. Many runners would chronically experience the same or a similar type of injury and not be able to identify why it consistently happened. Maintaining a log over a period of time allowed them to identify, for example, that every time they went on a particular hill climb, the next day they would have severe cramps. Sometimes they discovered that once they laundered their shoes or replaced a pair with the exact same model, they would have an ankle injury. The patterns revealed themselves through the consistency of the log.

When something appears to randomly or serendipitously go well, look for the patterns. You may find in the actions that repeat themselves across events that there are keys—patterns for continual success. In either case, whether to eliminate behavior or to continue a particular thing, it requires a conscious decision to go looking for repetitive patterns.

How might you identify your patterns?

The momentum to fulfill a promise comes easily once the decision is made to embrace the promise.

Ask a baseball player: once the bat leaves their shoulder, they will tell you the momentum is set to swing for that ball.

Every promise involves many decisions along the way. The most significant decision is the first one, the one that says yes to embracing the promise, like when the bat leaves your shoulder. Dr. Martina McGowan underscores this thus: *"Yes; once the goal is set, the promise made, the path is easier to embrace, and momentum to sustain."*

Perhaps you know someone who perennially holds the bat resting up on their shoulder; they just keep it there. It's part of the way they navigate the world. Perhaps they announce to you that they're going to write a book, or that they have a great idea and they're going to start a company, or that they are going to travel to a place they've always wanted to go. What do they actually have? Just a bat that they carry around everywhere slung on their shoulder.

What can you do to metaphorically lift the bat off your shoulder?

Consider the finest advice you give your friend and take it yourself.

It's commonly understood that some of the wisest advice is dispensed to one's best friend. Guidance crafted from research, rooted in experience, and offered with compassion is readily available to a beloved. And yet it often happens, I am forgetful of that very same counsel at the time that I need it most.

I was the employee first aid provider appointed by HR for the company intermural softball team. I was trained in first aid by my father, who held that same position at his own jobsite for over thirty years. My immediate response in an emergency was practical and helpful, and still is. Except when I am injured. Everything I know to do for others is subsumed into the pain and discomfort I am experiencing. Dear ones will remind me of helpful applications or ask if I have taken an anti-inflammatory, or if I've used ice or heat. They will pointedly ask me if I should see a doctor.

Applying to myself an outward impulse to help others directed by this particular question is a pivot point. How would I behave, what would I suggest for my very best friend? When I remember to ask this and then follow with that exact action on my own behalf, everything proceeds more easily for me.

Will you consider using this question as a decision metric today?

Am I confusing knowing about this with knowing how to make it happen?

Decades ago, I started a story about a fictional cartographer who lived alone on the side of a hill. His house was the only structure visible for hundreds of miles. Travelers from all over the world stopped there for rest and food. In exchange, this character interviewed each visitor regarding all the ways of their journey. Over the decades, the cartographer built a library of extraordinarily useful maps. He did not know how to get to the places, yet he knew a lot about them. Over the years of charting these hundreds of locations, he had neglected to ask the guests how they traveled from where they began their journey to happening upon the house on the side of the hill. He rarely left his dwelling, yet was sought out as a location expert. He knew so much about the geography and other characteristics of faraway lands but knew next to nothing about how to get to them and back home again.

Jean Robin Martell confesses, *"This is very enlightening. I often set goals without a plan on how to make them happen. Herein could be one reason I don't reach them. I wouldn't set out on a road trip knowing only the destination and not the route to get there. I will think about this more and about how to incorporate a process more than just a final destination."*

There are some systems that allow for extensive study and mastery without any action being required. An example of this is writing a superior business plan. A document of this nature may very well qualify someone for a business loan. Knowing how to write the plan and knowing how to guide and grow the business that is the focus of the plan are two different matters entirely. Like the cartographer, a person can make inquiry of others and learn from people who have successfully operated a business. They will tell you their business hardly looks like the enterprise they first imagined. In an interview like this, remember to ask, "How did you have the courage to begin?" And ask, "How did you get from your beginning to where you are now?"

How do you differentiate between things you know something about versus things that you know how to initiate?

149 | *Who would want to sponsor or support this?*

There is a phrase that is so common I cannot specify the first time I heard it: If you don't ask, the answer is always no.

Nora Roberts, author, expands on that thought, "If you don't go after what you want, you'll never have it. If you don't ask, the answer is always no. If you don't step forward, you are always in the same place."

A friend took me to a fundraising event. She knew the focus was dear to my heart, one of inspiring young people to raise their sights in life through writing and reading. A young man, a rising star in the organization, delivered the organization's fundraising pitch. He was visibly anxious to the point of being obviously uncomfortable. Afterward, I asked his permission to make an observation about his fundraising appeal. Here's the summary of what I said: *"You delivered numbers, meaningful statistics, and percentages relating to the impact of your program. These are all valid. Next time, make that information available on a handout. Use the time you have and your unique voice to tell the story of one student who iconically demonstrates the profound impact of your program. Engage your audience. Make it personal, because it is. And then tell them there are thousands of students just like the one you just described who need help—their help. Then ask them to support your work. Be specific. Give them tangible handles for which they can reach in order to sponsor and support your efforts. Ask in such a way that their natural and only answer is yes."* I emphasized that the opportunity to sponsor meaningful action is an honor, not an obligation; that he was giving the people in the audience the chance to make a difference in the lives of young people without having to do the actual work themselves! He told me that changed everything for him.

In 2014, when a student in the next county over from mine fatally shot four other students and then took his own life, I was devastated. I'd had the impulse a few years earlier to travel through several counties in my own region and teach my forty-five-minute journal keeping presentation. I had made a few calls, none of which were returned, and I didn't pursue it. Further, at the time, I didn't have the resources to make it happen on my own. I asked myself, *if that boy had the discovery tool of a vital journal practice in his life experience, would he have committed such a sorrowful and irrevocable act?* I shared my questions on social media and said I would go to any classroom within a day's drive of the last classroom in which I had taught and present the forty-five-minute curriculum that summarized my own childhood (and lifelong) journal practice. Who would help me? Two states, ten days, and hundreds of students and miles later, I had been sponsored to provide a journal, pens, and stickers to every student who wanted them. I asked and learned that lots of people wanted to sponsor and support the effort of my teaching journal writing to students—lots. I only know and can tell this story because at a single point in time, I had the courage to ask who would want to sponsor or support this. I spoke up for myself, and in doing so, was able to speak up for others.

How will you gather the nerve to ask for support for your effort?

150 | *Is there a part that already exists that I do not have to originate?*

"What has been will be again, what has been done will be done again, there is nothing new under the sun."
—Ecclesiastes 1:9

I walked the streets of Pompeii, preserved in startlingly accessible condition from the day in August, 79 AD, that Mount Vesuvius burned its legacy into every crevice of the thriving Roman city. I walked as if I knew where I was going. I entered roofless dwellings with a core understanding of what they were for: a bistro; a bakery. So much has changed over the many centuries regarding the *how* of things. However, the *why* of things remains very much the same.

Looking for a part that already exists so that I do not have to originate it applies to actual things as well as ideas and systems. If it is at least largely true that there is nothing new under the sun, then it becomes a matter of sleuthing, of research, to discover the necessary element that must be evident somewhere. This is a disruption of the assumption that if you don't have it, you have to go acquire it from somewhere specifically oriented toward providing that part.

My father was a heavy equipment production manager; my brother-in-law worked as a maintenance engineer for that same facility. They were tasked with keeping the machines in the place running to meet production quotas. Curiosity and innovation, paired with open-minded attention from these two, saved that company thousands of lost labor hours. Some of those machines were so old that the replacement parts were no longer readily available. They had to be resourceful in their search for parts, they had to ask and look in unlikely places. Finding where a part already existed was the quickest fix. Faced with having to create a part from scratch, I remember my brother-in-law telling me he'd found exactly the thing he needed, in abundance; he only had to carefully remove one little bit. An immediate solution was applied compared to waiting weeks for the precise part to be delivered. This translates as well to systems, ideas, and concepts. Just because an idea might feel new to you, it does not mean you must invent, or actually reinvent, every element. It's likely been done before, yes. The freshness, innovation, and disruption come, as it has never yet been done uniquely by you.

In a different generation, it was an honorable thing to make do and to use what was already present. A culture of commercial acquisition insists that one must get the newest, sparkliest thing in order to complete any sort of task. I will spend the remainder of my life unlearning this impulse.

And what about the realm of intellectual acquisition and innovation? It's tempting to believe that a new certification, a fresh training, or another degree is required in order to meet a specific project goal or solve a challenge.

What if…you already have or know what is required to solve a problem you are facing or create what you need? Then it becomes a matter of translating and transferring rather than acquiring. If this worked for that, then how can it be translated to this application that you are working with in the current context?

What if you already have what you need?

|5| Loving yourself precedes any effort at effectiveness.

If you operate from a lack of confidence, or if you have any degree of loathing directed at yourself, it will, absent any conscious effort on your part, impact every exchange. The impact of a person who loves and appreciates themselves is immediately obvious. Self-love masquerades in the professional world as confidence. People who have the confidence of self-love share common characteristics, among them:

- Attitudes emanate from the inside out and happiness begins within.
- Shaming is not in the tool kit.
- Learning, not judgment, is the priority.
- Being irreplaceable is not upheld as a goal.
- They grasp that their no is someone else's yes.
- Hard listening is at play, and they remember what they hear.
- Even in uncertainty, they speak with clarity.
- They are not tied to the grand gesture or that once-in-a-lifetime deal.
- They seek out and celebrate small wins.
- They practice wellness.
- They aren't afraid of the spotlight, and they share it happily when they are in it.
- They are willing to fail and willing to risk in order to create a resolution.
- They elevate others, knowing that a rising tide lifts all boats.
- They ask fearlessly for what they need.
- They will be absurd for the greater good.

Do you have a deep and consistent self-love? What might be different if you allowed your confidence to rise up?

Courage doesn't always get it right, not even the third time.

Courage is the capacity to bring it fresh to the field the tenth time knowing it was only a matter of time.

Ironically, the turning point of effective momentum is being brave enough to consider embracing moments of stillness.

Forward momentum; proximal direction; aim; productivity; movement toward specific aspirations—these are the societal targets that Western culture upholds as ideal. Doing; going; getting; more! The goal is always "better and faster." How often have you heard content teachers make the claim that they teach how to get more done in less time? When experiencing the pressure of all these calls to action, it takes grit to choose moments of stillness. It is a difficult choice to make in the midst of much to do and many promises to fulfill. But keep this in mind: Without stillness or a practiced pause, movement can tend toward being a hot mess, exhausted, and lacking clarity.

Think about the times when you've heard this exchange: "How are you?" "I'm swamped. I've got so much to do. I've worked so many days in a row." Much of Western culture teaches us to equate value with actions—with getting "it" done, whatever "it" might be. We have become willing to frame our own identities in the context of how much we *do*, how busy or fully occupied our days are.

Let's consider thinking time, the opportunity for reflection, quiet contemplation, and rest. While there is an academic case that is often made on behalf of the benefits of this kind of contemplative time, these concepts are not broadly extolled in real-life application. An old campaign for Coca-Cola featured the phrase, "The pause that refreshes." Even in that context, it involved acquiring and consuming a stimulating beverage. I always laugh at the more recently turned phrase, "Don't just do something, sit there!" There's a lifting effect in recognizing the importance of a pause, of the opportunity to rest or reflect. Meditation, yoga, and declared time off from social media or work activities notwithstanding, it's still not the norm in our communities.

It's unfortunate that sitting still has been conflated with doing nothing. Keen and purposeful pauses have produced some fine ideas. Stepping away, turning everything "off," and simply pausing is an extraordinary reset mechanism. When digital devices go wonky for no apparent reason, most often the easiest fix is to turn the thing off for a short bit and then restart it. It is a technological demonstration of the benefit of the pause that also applies to the human operating system. Productivity benefits from pausing.

Can you pair your forward movement with practiced pauses?

153 *If I had to draw this, what form might it take?*

I asked her to imagine what our project might look like; she declined. I said it was a simple exercise, just putting her ideal state of energy and momentum into a visual context, like a metaphor, only in form and in color. Again, she declined. Ordinarily, our work together was seamless and we had a cooperative flow. She could see that I was puzzled. Then, she told me. She has a condition called *aphantasia*. She is unable to play out images in her mind. So she can remember facts about her husband, but she cannot trace his jawline in her mind's eye. She is mentally blind.

Absent such a condition, attributing form to concepts and exchanges is exceptionally helpful. Drawing a visual of a challenge or a conflict, an ideal state of mind, how you would like an event to unfold, or how you would prefer to hold a memory can inform you in ways that just mentally considering it cannot. It is a significant tool to deepen your understanding.

Have a problem to solve? Draw it out and literally see what you will learn.

154 | *Allow fun to permeate the day. Laugh.*

Allow: To allow is a form of intentional welcome. Properly defined, it includes granting permission and providing the necessary time and opportunity for a thing.

To permeate is to spread throughout something. To permeate calls to mind the smell of vanilla and sugar wafting through a kitchen when sugar cookies are baking.

To allow fun to permeate a day recognizes the essential role fun and playfulness have in the pursuit of solving problems and the inclination toward innovation.

There's a very misleading statement that has circulated for some years and is attributed to many different authors: "Do what you love, and you'll never work a day in your life."

First, the phrase is disparaging to the noble craft of work. Second, it ignores the reality that most things have an element or two that aren't that lovable. (Cue music and remind anyone about the task of emptying the trash or washing the dishes that other people have left.)

Find ways to create an attitude of fun around even the least desirable of tasks. Laughter paves the shortest distance between undesirable chores.

What advantage can you see to inviting fun into the day?

155 | *There are roots of knowledge and experience in every growing concept.*

Roots; they are deep. Most often they are out of sight. This is how it can be with knowledge and experience. They are embedded in your being so that you easily overlook them or even forget they are there.

A client just shared that she's freezing up in grad school because she's in a class that reminds her of a course she failed in college—thirty years ago. She's had thirty years since that failure to collect skills and successes, knowledge and experience. Perhaps what she is facing now is new to her. Still, there are things like it; she now has transferable applicable skills that could be brought to bear on her struggle. And she will perhaps remember that *this* is not *that*. This challenge in the now is not equivalent to her failure of then.

Can you hear the thing whisper, "You know so much more than seems evident to you"?

Look deeply. Will you look even deeper still for the roots you already have that will help you grow this new thing?

156 | *Surprise waits in the most ordinary and familiar of things.*

What in this could possibly surprise me? Connie Bennett uses this question in the context of many different circumstances. This becomes an excellent antidote to oh-no-ing or catastrophizing. When the default is to assume the worst, pull this question out of your resilience tool kit.

Pain, depression, and fatigue provide a wide swath of real estate on which one can stand and expect the worst. Because, well, the worst just keeps showing up in some phases of life. Especially when it is all you are used to experiencing.

It takes some amount of courage when one is part of a group that is given to catastrophizing to be the one who pipes up with a positive possibility, the chance of a pleasant surprise. Do a gut check and have the capacity to ask. Sometimes we actually get to see what we expect to see. And when what we expect is a delightful surprise, it shows up (not always, but sometimes).

Go ahead, ask. Ask that question at least once today.

What might happen if you are willing to find surprise?

157 | *Looking for potential benefits is a good default position.*

I have a friend who likes to counter gloomy negative assessments with some version of, "Let's imagine what else could possibly go right."

If in the moment, I am being the negative one, this response can be somewhat annoying. In spite of potentially being or feeling annoying, it is an excellent call to a broader accountability in consideration and thinking. However, if I'm in a strategy session, I love balancing the requisite planning tools of preparing options in case things go wrong with working to identify potential benefits that may have escaped notice.

It seems to be a component or a natural impulse of human nature to automatically imagine all of the negative potentials that don't yet exist, imagining all the things that might possibly go wrong. Training to see as yet unidentified benefits, all that could go right, is an outstanding skill.

Discovering and identifying potential benefits is a great reason to pass an idea around to a couple of innovative thinkers, in addition to your own thinking, of course!

In addition to yourself, who might you ask to identify potential benefits?

What is keeping you from the next step?

A bazillion things might be keeping you from the next step. Some of them are so embedded in your stories that they require spelunking to even put light on them. What is keeping you from the next step? People enter therapeutic relationships to untangle the threads and fibers of their resistance. If that is not an option for you at this time, there is a practice that might be helpful. I've used it with good results for decades. What is it? Letter writing!

Here are two approaches that use the practice of writing a letter to understand your resistance to a thing, get to a level of clarity, and determine what comes next.

- Call to mind that dearest friend of yours, the friend for whom you would do almost anything. Imagine *them* in the circumstance of resisting their next step. Write them a letter offering your best advice. Then, take the advice.

- Use your vivid imagination to personify the thing that you are keeping yourself from or resisting. Allow the next step or your resistance to the next step to write you a letter. Just push your pen or dance your fingers on your keyboard and give in to your imagination. Allow whimsy to enlighten you as to what either of these things would have to say to you. Write it out and then read it out!

What *is* keeping you from the next step?

The capacity to reframe a circumstance can be a marvel.

It can shift perspective and allow hosts of refreshing potentials to blow through a dusty space. Reframing loves to ask, "What else could be true?"

Reframing can also be dangerous and debilitating. In this context, one forgets Maya Angelou's sage admonition, "When someone first shows you who they are, believe them." Instead, an unacceptable circumstance is reframed into a transitional experience. That transitional experience sounds like, "next time will be better." The danger? The next time that the untenable condition continues, the reframe is already primed for the next, next time. And you know, that story just keeps on going!

The fabulous place for a reframe to exist is in your own perspective and about your own experience. How does that go?

A morning when dawn might be greeted with a groan and a temptation to roll over is reframed to, "I get to do this _____ today and then I'll reward myself with _____." Or maybe the reframe occurs while you are rolled over and after you finished groaning!

Will you look inside and see where you can healthfully and generously reframe something today?

**Promise to allow goodness
to soar within your soul.**

It is essential to craft a courteous and compassionate process of self-talk in order to allow goodness to soar within your soul. Sometimes you need a cheerleader rather than a drill sergeant.

In my most challenged, despairing moments, I can talk to myself in a tone or manner that I would never use with anyone else—ever.

Caren Albers observes, *"This is one thing I know for sure. To soar in your days requires mastering compassionate self-talk. Being that soft place to land at night, cuddled in your own arms, as you repeat the story of your day reminding yourself you did the best you could and believing it. Before I go to sleep, I say, 'I love you, Caren.' Sometimes I answer back, 'I love you, too.' Try it! (But don't say* Caren *because that would be weird.)"*

I've taken to addressing myself tenderly as, "Honey girl," when I am inclined to start in with credible but critical assessments or divisive commentary. Instead of accusations, I feed myself the inquiry, "What's really going on here, honey girl?" "Is there an unmet need here?" "Did you try your best?" "Are you feeling fearful of something?"

A beloved friend often calls me to ask, "Are you treating my fine friend exceptionally well today?" Of course, she's asking about me!

How do you allow goodness to soar within your soul? Will you help yourself soar?

161 | *Consider the difference between looking and seeing.*

It happened recently. I opened my spice cupboard looking for a specific spice. I looked. I looked again. Nope. How is it possible it was not there? I had recently used it. I live alone. Without opposable thumbs, I was certain Webster wasn't the culprit. Slightly annoyed, I closed the cupboard and poured myself some mineral water. I scanned the counters. Nope; no misplaced spice jar.

I decided to look one more time. I reminded myself of my best editing trick, which is to read the page from the bottom to the top. It helps me notice misspelled words I have overlooked based upon automatically filling in what I know they're supposed to be.

So this time, I looked first where the jar was never placed and was never meant to be, the cupboard version of the bottom of the page. Looking where I did not expect to see the spice jar allowed me to observe what I had previously overlooked: the spice jar, right in front of my nose! Not returned to the place where I usually put it, but pretty darn close. The phrase, "If it was a snake, it would have bit me," applies here. In spite of having looked twice, that fresh approach allowed me to see what I was looking for.

Can you notice the difference for you today between looking and seeing?

162 | *Does a model for this already exist?*

The desire for originality has fostered a lot of reinvention. Even with a relatively original or untried premise, there may exist some iteration of it somewhere in the world. With the globe virtually at one's fingertips via the Internet, there's every reason to invest some time into researching a project or idea before deciding to start from scratch. Even when using already established models, you bring your own parameters to every endeavor. Incorporating existing baselines and building upon the discoveries of others may shorten your timeline and deliver results along the way that you cannot even now imagine.

Will you allow existing structures to assist you as you build your idea today?

163 | *Is comparing myself now to my own past performance inhibiting my next steps?*

"This is how I do it." Comparing my own past performance to a next step in the present moment can reinforce a habit or can inspire change.

I took a hard look at my spice cupboard. One spice, a gift from a friend, is the lone exception; all the other spices are known and I am comfortable cooking with them. I have an impulse to learn new things that involves culinary shifts. New spices and a new cookbook are on their way! Considering a performance comparison opportunity

Courage Doesn't Always Roar...

provides a metric for evaluating a change. It can mark progress or it can reveal decline.

As you consider your own path, rather than letting past performance motivate or determine your next steps, can you consider an aspirational goal to inspire a different way forward?

164 | *Do I want credit or results?*

Both are nice! And both can be the aspirational objective. The answer depends upon the core desired outcome. If your only objective is to add a specific, measurable accomplishment to your résumé for an upcoming promotion or interview, then having credit is significant. In many other instances, the results matter as much or much more than getting credit.

As a young, female executive in an industry governed by men, I traded credit for results frequently and intentionally. I knew that feeding a plan through a middle-aged, white male would win board approval almost instantly. I rarely got credit, except with the single middle-aged white male presenting my plan. In spite of not getting recognition for my idea, I often got gratifying results. When I determined that it was important to teach those who were keen to dismiss the systems presented by a young woman, I made sure to speak up and speak out. I maintained a private paper trail in case getting credit ever became an issue. When the metric is results-driven rather than measured by fairness or acknowledgement, then the choice becomes more easily defined.

Observe today if you must make a choice between results or credit.

165 | *Within a single human dwell many different capacities and expressions.*

Brandie Sellers, in her practice as an open-hearted therapist, often asks, *"Which part of my personality is driving this decision?"* This question has the promise of aligning the client with, or at least leading the client to become more aware of, their motivation.

There's only one you, unique and whole. Your personality drives different vehicles depending on the destination and the nature of the road you are traveling.

I just made a decision driven by my needs as an introvert. If I had allowed the part of me that thrives on connection and discovery to carry the day, I would've made a significantly different decision. Knowing that, I am able to see that neither decision is less than the other, and certainly neither choice is wrong; each is simply driven by a different part of my personality.

Can you consciously be aware of a specific part of your personality that drives a decision today?

Are there advantages or concessions that I have yet to negotiate or ask for?

I paid my corporate lawyer and accountant to provide their best guidance. They had. Consistently. In two different instances their advice was counter to a plan of mine. Independently they both told me the things I had in mind were impossible. My simple response was: "It's always NO unless you ask." It was met with a patronizing tolerance. In both instances, after I negotiated what they considered undoable, they laughingly told me I should've been a lawyer instead of an artist. I told them it was my creativity that gave me the foundation for artful negotiation.

I made a substantial purchase. The seller automatically invoiced the purchase in installments. I asked if there was a financial advantage to paying for the purchase all at once. Yes, there was, and was it ever a substantial savings! I wouldn't have been aware of it if I hadn't asked.

Conversely, I have had experiences where my suggested concessions were rejected immediately. I have lived lots of narratives where I have been reluctant to even ask or enter a negotiation. I've noticed some things about myself at times when I am resistant to seeking advantage or entering a negotiation...

- I doubt myself or my own sense of worth, and I am uncertain if I merit being an exception
- I've already formed a negative scenario of the likely outcome ("It's too late, they won't have a ticket left")

- I lack fire or passion regarding the specific outcome I am seeking

Do you already have a standard inquiry that you use on a regular basis? Could you use it today? If you do not have an inquiry that allows you to seek advantage, can you create one that feels comfortable to you?

167 | *The actual stride of an individual can be a tip off to their mindset.*

It's an oft used assessment: "She seemed to take it in stride."

It means that in spite of potential upset or obstacle, a person's natural gait or walk was not interrupted or impacted. Perhaps you have said these words, "It stopped me in my tracks." That is the opposite of your natural stride, which is a rhythm rooted in the physical world. We embody our intention in the manner we proceed and navigate. Our stride broadcasts a mood, an intention, and even a potential action.

Cheryl Marks Young observes, *"I believe with a change of focus, we change our stride and change our results. And sometimes it happens without us realizing it, like the story of a marathon runner who viewed his running as work, so that he had to literally psyche himself up to do each race. Then one day, he used a presenting technique that had him appreciate his surroundings while he ran rather than focusing on the hard work ahead of him in the race. At the end of the race, he realized he'd made his best time and truly felt lighter as he had actually enjoyed the scenery and the journey. I believe we can walk or run better by connecting to our most natural stride along the way."*

Connecting to the cadence of your natural stride is the body affirming the presence of flow.

Is it possible to change the experience of the day by connecting to your most natural stride as you walk through your moments?

168 | *Memory can comfort or cause crisis; memory can be a source of contention or a data point.*

Memory is a funny thing. Even seconds after a thing happens, memory starts the work of rewriting the event in order for it to align with our unique perception and bias.

Comfort. A scent is carried on a warm autumn's evening wind. It brings back the days of return to school and the smell of new shoes. A long-held memory is now refreshed.

Crisis. In facing a remembered event, courage can be required. There are many memories that are painful and tender, and they hide in a corner trying to avoid the light of attention and recollection. Bringing them into the daylight and evaluating their place in the present moment requires a particular fortitude.

Contention. Memory is a source of contention represented by an exchange containing these words: "That's not how I remember it." A bias will insert words that were never uttered and fabricate an intention that was actually never held. The same event attended by the same five people will exist in memory in five distinctly different ways.

A Data Point. Memory identifies patterns. Memory allows learning. Recalling a wrong turn helps the driver the next time to take the turn that leads to the desired destination. Remembering something that was done correctly and with innovation allows that success to be repeated.

Memory behaves in many different ways. Watch yours. Every space is a learning place, and everywhere one goes is an opportunity to grow.

Can you check for the accuracy and effectiveness of your remembered experience?

169 | *There are optimum conditions that allow you to lean into your life and learn from it.*

I have two very different ways of being a learner. The first approach is willing and curious; this aspect is a voracious consumer of new information and an enthusiastic but unmasterful applier of the new knowledge. The second type is reluctant and weary and shakes a fist at the impersonal sky, declaring, "I just want a quiet day! Enough learning and growing for the moment."

Even in the fist-shaking there is learning. When a large pitcher of water pours into a small glass, it doesn't take long for the glass to overflow. Human capacity, although different for each person, does have an overflow point. Technically, the brain requires rest (including sleep) to efficiently transfer short-term data into long-term memory. Without that, the mind becomes that small glass, perennially overflowing. When occupying that second learning space, remembering to rest and restore yourself is an essential part of being able to learn. This needed replenishing of mental resources also increases the capacity to seize opportunities to learn and grow.

Have you restored your being adequately to be able to lean into learning?

170 | *In all things dwells the chance to learn.*

It's practical to just pause when standing in a place of unknowing. Stop. Ask. Do research. Defer a step to a better informed time and place. Sometimes that pause is the best decision. And other times? Maintain a cautious optimism while asking, "What might this teach me along the way?"

Being a willing student, both vulnerable and open, presents gifts that are unknowable in the moment of choosing to move forward, deciding to continue along the way. It's tempting to want to know everything before proceeding—or at least to want to know a lot more than is known at the present moment. It's not possible to know everything, and it is even difficult to know almost everything. In the television show *NCIS*, the forensic scientist, a character called Abby Sciuto, was asked what she was looking for when she was examining evidence. Her reply asserted that she never knew what she was looking for, and that, in fact, she aggressively worked toward not expecting to find anything. That open-minded looking allowed her to more accurately see the unexpected—which was most often exactly what she needed to solve the case!

Believing that we need to know everything or close to everything before proceeding means we might miss the most important thing we could learn. Can I make it safe to explore the hidden places?

When a small area needs to be explored in the context of mining, a machine called an auger is used. It is mobile and can be managed by one person. If you can imagine a jackhammer merged with a handheld drill and enlarged, you have a pretty good picture of an auger.

For deeper and more significant excavation like drilling for oil, a rig is required. It cannot drill immediately to the depth required to extract the desired commodity. It must drill distance by distance and use a mud pump to remove the slurry, the waste matter generated by the drilling. The deeper the drill goes, the harder it is to remove the unnecessary material. A casing has to be inserted to help raise up and remove the levels of excavated earth. This makes it possible to clear a space to hoist up and drop down the pipes necessary to extract the oil.

This mechanical process is an amazing metaphor for safely exploring opportunities for learning that are carried deep within ourselves, an event or exchange. In some instances, an auger will meet the needs of the experience. In other circumstances, supports and additional systems are necessary to go to the depth required to extract the essential matter. Everything in life is a classroom opportunity.

What tools can you use to excavate the most valuable lessons from all your experiences?

|7| *Every encounter plays a part in the curriculum of your life experience.*

If I allow everyone I encounter today to be a teacher, and if I permit each experience to join the faculty of my Life University, then I am (for sure) getting full value for my enrollment—my engagement in this day.

Gaining new knowledge and deepening the grasp of existing structures is a pleasure when circumstances are pleasant. A different kind of scholarship occurs when in exchange with a difficult person or a less-than-ideal incident. Extracting value from the most unwelcome event redeems the unpleasantness. If everything today represents teachable moments, then the next natural question is, "What might I learn from this?"

The nature of resilience has been an active matter of scientific and psychological study for over one hundred years. I suspect that the author of *Mindset*, Carol Dweck, found much of her research in this arena. There are those who become mired in crisis and paralyzed by it (a fixed mindset) and those who find every crisis and challenge an opportunity to learn and deepen their skills (a growth mindset).

In the middle of the last century, the study of resilience was largely occupied with challenged populations. Researchers were asking what moves some people out of poverty while others remain locked into those conditions. Each successive decade has seen the study expand to cover virtually all population segments. It's a broad field of study with numerous books available. Generally, there are key components associated with resilience; one among them that is controversial is that there is a genetic predisposition toward resilience. Characteristics decidedly not held in one's DNA include: at least one dependably supportive relationship, flexible and adaptive skill building, and positive experiences from which unique and personal coping skills are learned and repeatedly applied.

Where will you look for your capacity for resilience?

172 | *Do not become absorbed by the trivial.*

I was on my way to sort and organize a drawer when I rediscovered the precise papers I had been looking for. I wanted to manage an artful process for a particular project. My drawer organization task delayed, I started in on my Shibori paper dying project.

The trivial is often attractive to me. It is immediately gratifying. I love placing checkmarks by easy tasks, declaring them *done*—so rewarding. To the more practical, linear observer, it could appear that I had abandoned the matter of consequence—organization—for the messy triviality of starting an art practice.

Nope.

When I wonder how it is I want to live each day and therefore how it is that I ultimately wish to be remembered, "she was wildly creative" comes to mind. In no imagined eulogy ever does it occur to me to include the words, "she maintained tidy and organized drawers."

Immediately I will add that tidiness would've helped me find those papers a lot sooner. Certainly organization, depending upon priority, timing, and need is also a matter of consequence.

What if you look for something that appears trivial that may turn out to be pivotal to matters of consequence?

173 | *What are the consequences of attempting to control something that's not mine to control?*

Perhaps you've heard the phrase, "Not my circus, not my monkeys." I've said for years, "My no becomes someone else's yes." This concept can be tracked back to the Stoic philosophers of several thousand years ago. It's been iterated in modern times from coaches to comedians to children to chaplains.

Control is illusory. There's only one thing over which there's any control at all, and even that seems at times somewhat unpredictable!

That one thing is how one chooses to respond—to anything. Planners, perfectionists, players—all have a desire to control elements and outcomes. Apparent randomness and impersonal surprise thwart those plans repeatedly. Grasping tightly to the illusion of control is an invitation to chronic frustration. Self-knowing partners well with flexibility and resilience for more contented days.

What may go differently if you relinquish a sense of control over a particular thing?

174 | *In a natural result of responding to what we focus on, we begin to become like the people we most admire.*

I was primarily without adult supervision as a teen. My mom had died, and my dad operated on a predictable cycle which involved graveyard shift Sunday night through Thursday, followed each weekday by a shift of drinking until his bedtime between four and five in the afternoon. Weekends were spent by myself in town or sometimes at the river house with my father. My closest family had family of their own and checked on me as often as possible. I navigated the unfamiliar and unknown by asking myself, "How would I act if I knew how to do this?" This morphed into, "What if I pretended this was easy?" I didn't know that I was cultivating the basis for a decision in the direction of self-reliance, yet that is what was happening. I was blessed to have youth

Courage Doesn't Always Roar...

leaders and teachers I admired and of whom could make inquiry. I was lost lots of the time and always found my literal way home and my metaphorical way back to myself. Ultimately, these young experiences helped me to become someone I admired and respected. What would I (at my best) do? WWID?

Eleanor Roosevelt died when I was five. I was unaware of her as a historical figure and dramatic global influencer until my junior year of high school. In my American history class, she was barely an offhand reference in relationship to FDR's presidency. I found a keen interest in her life story that continues to this day. I have asked myself for decades, "What would Eleanor do?" WWED?

I have a circle of very strong women friends. I am blessed in that way. Each of them has a unique set of strengths that I admire and know so well that I can often call upon their assistance without actually having to call upon them in real time. I often find myself asking, "What would Kathleen do?" This is a question that has served me very well. WWKD?

Who is or who are your (fill in the blank) in this question…

"What would _____ do?"

In what circumstance can you apply a behavior of someone that you most admire?

There is a remarkable synergy between intelligence and intuition.

There is a field of cognitive and behavioral research that asserts that intelligence/intuition as resources in decision-making should be joined by *and*, not with *or*. It's called Naturalistic Decision Making. NDM is a field of study formally registered in 1989. In summary, it suggests that experience, expertise, and tacit knowledge all conspire to frame the best decisions. Unaware of this field, I'd called this process "informed intuition" for decades. Shawn Patrick Rivera affirms this from his own experience, saying, "I love this so much! After doing a lot of work around listening to my intuition, it now helps validate the decisions and ideas that form in my mind. When you know, you know. I suspect as those experiences deepen, I will also find the reverse to be true, with my intuition driving more of my conscious decisions."

The function of head and heart have long been required to stand independent of each other. In the NDM model, they are each half of a single whole.

Which of your decisions may benefit from the synthesis of these two readily available resources?

Waiting for perfection may mean waiting a very long time.

Ancient wise ones have been answering this question for years: Is waiting for perfection awaiting something that is unrealistic? Can I live with the imperfect? A friend of mine finished his novel in his thirties. He spent three decades polishing it up before self-publishing it at age sixty-five.

Voltaire famously said the best is the enemy of the good. Confucius asserted, "Better a diamond with a flaw than a pebble without." Shakespeare chimed in, writing that in striving to better things, "oft we mar what's well."

Did my friend's fictional account get any better over the thirty years that he spent editing it repeatedly? Perhaps it did. It certainly occupied large swaths of his time and attention. Ask anyone who sat near him at an event. It's what he preferred to talk about for thirty years. Perhaps that is what served him best. I sometimes wonder what stories he might have spun if he had released his tale into the world after the first couple of times it was edited. I was the one who transcribed his handwritten notes on the first iteration. It was a good story, perhaps not "best," but good.

Modern teachers and trainers talk about the 10,000 hours required for mastery of a thing. Perhaps if I had thought about perfection and 10,000 hours when I was getting ready to start my art company, I might not have started. After these decades, when I look back, I realize the things that I love doing most likely have had 10,000 hours inadvertently packed into them. Just recently I've had three digital conversations with an industry peer preparing for an upcoming event. It's a short event, and by its nature, it is casual. The most recent times, she asked if I thought more preparation would be an advantage, saying that she wanted to be fully prepared. I responded that it's important for her to remember she's been preparing her whole life for this brief event!

I think many great things fall into the abyss of working toward perfection. The expectation of the perfect thing is mightily unrealistic. Every day gives plenty of training in living with imperfection. I'll emphasize it again, plenty! Many of my advance readers agree, and each affirm an element of the truth of this.

Martina McGowan: *"Absolutely. Pursuing perfection is a trap. Embrace what is. Find the beauty there; there is almost always something good. And if it is not as 'beautiful' as you'd like, try to do something, one thing (at a time) to improve it."*

Pam Williams: *"One of the greatest gifts my wife, Marci, gave me was helping me to let go of the need for perfection. Sometimes I still stubbornly clung to old habits, but she had such an awesome way of reminding me that there was so much to be experienced in the world that spending time on perfection where it didn't matter (unlike with brain surgery, or flying a plane, for example) took time away from other beautiful adventures and experiences that were waiting. She helped me learn how to throw a very relaxed dinner party. I'm grateful every day for this wisdom she brought to my life. I'll carry it into the next chapter."*

Kathleen Gallagher Everett: *"This resonates with me so much. Becoming an Olympic athlete or a master chef or a violinist or a neurosurgeon requires aspiration to perfection. While it may not be achievable, the level of accomplishment would not be attained without that striving. Applying that standard to everything, however, is a recipe for discontent. I am glad your friend stayed true to his goal and hope it was because that's what he truly wanted for the finished product. I would prefer to have generated one stellar work than ten mediocre ones, but that's my preference. I struggle with this and work to cultivate the discernment needed to find sweet balance. The answer may lie not in the fact of our striving for the best possible outcome, but in why we do it: the difference between striving for our own 'perfect' because it brings joy vs. doing so because we feel wholly inadequate or judged for anything less."*

Caren Albers: *"Perfection is a myth and the spoiler of the 'good enough.' Which is by definition is good enough. I think the word 'enough' plays a leading role here. When we feel like we are enough we stop trying for more."*

Maxine Rothman: *"My practice is to embrace* wabi sabi—*to find the beauty in imperfection. Good. Enough. (My brain always sees these as two separate notions, with emphasis on the pause of the period.)"*

What might be different for you if you purposely apply the measure of *good enough* today?

177 | *Considering energy as the single most valuable human asset changes every perspective.*

What is consuming too much energy? This is a question that CPA and coach Sharon Martinelli has asked herself and her clients for decades.

Understanding the expenditure of human energy can be a difficult concept. The most obvious metric for me is in a conversation with another human being. After engaging with some people, I feel invigorated; I feel as if my level of get-up-and-go has been restored to an exceptionally high level. In other instances, after speaking with different people, I end up feeling as if I need a nap. My level of available energy is measurably depleted, if not almost exhausted. You've heard the humorous saying, "My get-up-and-go just got up and went!" Those are two real-life instances of my capacity to measure my own consumption of energy.

Christine Miserandino, a New Yorker with an autoimmune disorder, once explained her condition to her best friend when they were in college eating in a diner. When asked to describe how it felt to have lupus, she clarified that on some days, she was active and fully participative, and other days, she could barely get out of bed—and in both instances, she never looked sick. Christine was inspired to grab all the "spoons" within her reach. With a handful of physical spoons on the table, she explained to her friend that a spoon represents a consistent measure of energy. Unlike a healthy person who feels as if they have an unlimited supply of energy at the start of the day, a person with an autoimmune disorder or another invisible disease has a finite supply of energy. Each day, that individual must choose how or where that energy is invested. Christine's spoon theory has been widely shared over the years and helps some people understand better when someone says, "I just don't have the spoons for tonight's party."

There is emerging research that expands on a larger truth: No human supply of energy is limitless. Everyone's reservoir is different, and the size of an individual's energy supply may even vary from day to day, or even depending on the time of day. Human energy is not like the electric company's credits if you have solar panels, or like a battery. Human energy is renewable more than it is storable. Just as a battery can be recharged, a human's energy depleted at the end of one day can be restored by exercise, nutrition, or good sleep and readied for the next day.

Using Miserandino's metaphor as a model, build your own metric using an icon that has meaning for you. "We build the book of our lives by the stories we write in each day." If you have seventeen measures of energy at the start of your day and that supply needs to last all day, how will you invest them? There is emerging research on a concept called "ego depletion" indicating that willpower has a fatigue level, and there's research supporting the idea that the capacity for making sound decisions is also finite, although those theories are not yet universally accepted within the behavioral science community. My own experience validates them with a frequent explanation of a poor choice being, "I must've been really tired." Kathleen Gallagher Everett adds, *"I have made a practice of paying attention to what I am spending my energy on—if I am fretting, resentful, or continuing to carry old baggage, that all takes energy to maintain, like a storage unit. If I start the day in the red because of the old junk I continue to finance, I won't have as much to spend on meaningful and purposeful work. It's definitely finite."*

Applied in the course of the day, this means that what may take one metric of energy such as a spoon in the morning hours of my experience may consume three or four in the evening after a full day of expending my available willpower energy. For years, people have just shrugged their shoulders and said without fully understanding, "I don't know what happened. All of a sudden I just seemed to run out of steam." That, of course, draws on an old mechanical reference: Picture a train operated under the power of steam that is suddenly without the force of fire creating steam behind it, stopped still on the tracks—no "go."

Your available energy is your personal banking institution for what you get to spend and invest energetically in your day.

Is there a time of day that would ideally use less energy (spoons) than any other? Will any particular activity add to your energy endowment for the day?

178 | *A key to success in this day is to dwell on all the things that could go right.*

In the face of challenge or even danger, the impulse can be toward anxiety, toward "what if," toward all the possible things that could go wrong. Such a response, rooted in fear, constricts. It constricts vision and breathing—every body response tightens. Fear fulfills a significant role: it points out when there is an authentic threat and alerts one to the need to protect. But often fear takes its job too far. Instead of simply serving as a warning system, it seeds the imagination with increasingly growing doomsday scenarios. Fear does not unfold a map of numerous alternative routes. Instead, it walks the mind's eye down only one road: all the things that could go wrong. It is inevitably a road featuring every possible dismal, dangerous, undesirable outcome.

Dwelling on all the things that could go right must not imply denial, rather a willingness to accept that many possibilities exist in a single experience. You may legitimately be concerned about falling/failing... But beside every fear of falling exists the possibility of flying...

These are anticipatory views, crafting a speculative future on the art bench of your mind and body. Asking or allowing for what could go right is an appropriate companion to initial fear. Contained in Talmudic traditions and within the teachings of the Stoic philosophers down through time to modern psychology is this: We see what we think we will see. It's frequently referred to as confirmation bias.

Our expectations drive our perception. Psychologists have studied "motivated perception" for decades. Across disciplines and centuries, informed observers agree that we dwell on or see that which we wish or expect to see.

Instead of defaulting to only all the things that might go wrong, what might result if, at least, you pursued the corresponding inquiry, "What could go right?"

179 *The wise see within the difficulty the very thing that helps them thrive and grow.*

What promotes growth and thriving? The universal answer to this question is the thing that most people consciously try to avoid: difficulty.

All of us face difficulty—loss, obstacles, setbacks, crisis, and failures in the completion of what we intend. Ask just about any successful person to chart their key and proven life philosophies, and the answer will most likely thread through things in life that they have utilized keen resilience to overcome. Resilience gets lots of attention. It's not complicated. When resilient people encounter an obstacle, rather than giving up, they go in, they go through, and they get out. Even knowing when to step aside from a conflict is an element of resilience and a key to growth in itself.

As a student in the University of Life, you have the opportunity to learn from others who have grown through hardship. That is a good way to get a life lesson. It is, however, inevitable that you will experience detours and roadblocks of your own. When you know what it is that helps you grow, you are able to see these things as lessons, not limitations.

Embracing these less stellar elements of our lives allow us to learn to *thrive*, a word originating from the old Norse *thrifa*, meant to grasp, to get ahold of. The word morphed into *thrifask*, and by the time it was pressed into service in middle English, it was *thrive*, understood to mean grow or increase. Interestingly, the very same root word developed into thrift, thrifts, and thrifty. It meant prosperity, acquired wealth, and success. It's an archaic reference now, but savings institutions used to be called "thrifts."

In whole, to thrive means growth, expansion, to move toward and to realize a specific goal—especially in spite of obstacles or setbacks. Thrive reflects vigorous and dynamic growth and can be applied to almost anything that has the capacity for growth, especially when the "in spite of" is present.

Will you allow your experience of the difficult to shift by recognizing that within it exists the opportunity to grow and the ability to resiliently thrive?

Courage is not always in motion.

Sometimes it is the strength to pause, to stop, or to walk away.

One need not hold the thing in order to hold the memory.

I was not yet twenty-three years old and was in the midst of the kindest possible leaving of my childhood friend. Each searching for our own version of home, we had neglected to compare notes in advance of getting married to each other. We had barely earned the right to vote and were several years away from being able to take a legal drink when we said "yes" to each other. I have nothing physical from that period of time, and yet I still hold many memories.

It was a child's tea cup and saucer. My mother told me often that it had come into her collection of tea cups when I was born. Somehow I managed to preserve it for my own when her goods were largely dispersed to others when she died at fifty-seven, as I was just beginning adolescence. It moved with me many times until the move when Maureen, my high school pal, helped me move into a small apartment in Portland, Oregon.

She was earnest and ready to be helpful when she pulled a pile of crumpled packaging out of a box. That cup and saucer flew across the kitchen, cartoon style. The porcelain seemed suspended as we both held our breath, and then it crashed into dozens of pieces that skidded willy-nilly across the floor. She knew they were precious, and she burst into uncontrollable tears. The words I spoke then are the words written at the top of this page. I still hold the memory, and when I close my eyes, I can see the cup's fragile, petite handle and baby rose pattern.

What memory do you currently hold about a thing that is no longer in your possession?

|8| *Appreciate the practiced pause.*

"I will get back to you on that." "I want to discuss this at a time that is not now."

I have a well-deserved appreciation for the practiced pause. Even a pause for a few seconds contributes to a better decision or more desirable outcome. The pause invites my purposeful response to anger, for example, allowing me a rational moment to decide to release my rage or to walk a different way and thoughtfully explore my response.

Words matter. And once spoken, they rarely disappear.

The practiced pause aligns my intentions to my immediate experience. One of my most helpful maxims applies in the pause. "How is it I want to remember this? Now, act accordingly."

Here is a pragmatic example of a practiced pause. I most often leave online purchases in their shopping cart overnight or even for a few days. I frequently conclude that I don't actually require the purchase after all. The pause delivers results!

Another practical application of a pause impacts your working style. When experiencing a block on a project, even more than working on something unrelated, going for a five- or ten-minute walk or engaging in some outdoor physical activity is just the thing! If it's storming outside and a walk is not possible, a break is still beneficial.

Dance. Stand up and stretch. Even flapping your arms is a helpful physical activity.

Taking a brisk walk stimulates the parts of the brain that are dedicated to focus and attention. The movement becomes a mood elevator and a booster shot to creativity. Changing your focus to another project is also a helpful pause. Come away from that which frustrates you and feels unsolvable. When you return after a short physical activity, you will come back unstoppable.

In what ways can you test and apply the practiced pause?

182 | *Things get dropped. Not everything that is dropped is yours to pick up.*

Not every story that a friend tells requires a solution. Often a need is met in the focused act of simply listening to their story. When an individual is embroiled in a challenge, having the chance to be genuinely heard is their key to finding the door to their own solution. I practice several things to keep myself from my chronic impulse to immediately offer a solution.

This is a modest twist on the solution-offering classic response of, "Have you tried _____ <insert potential solution here>" instead transforming it into an inquiry: "What have you done or tried to deal with this?"

Leanore Curran shares, *"I used to be a chronic fixer-upper, and I offered way too much unsolicited advice. Now, I try to listen more and use better techniques to offer help."* A good question to ask is: "Please let me know how I can help you, or if you need anything."

Here are some other alternatives to the impulse of attempting to solve an issue for a friend:

- Ask their intention. "Do you need a safe space to just talk this through yourself, or do you want my input or ideas?"
- Be a witness first. Acknowledge that you have heard. "This sounds so hard. I can tell this is hurtful."
- Frame questions that invite their own answers to rise up rather than immediately offering your own.
- Recognize that simply listening can be the exact solution that someone really needs.

How will you look for a chance to fully listen to someone today?

183 | *Pursue or pause, start up or stop. Take a break or break out.*

In a world full of all kinds of noise and plenty of shouting, reader Deborah Dineen asks, *"Can I pause and breathe in the whispers?"* Even in a conundrum that swirls and lacks clarity, there are intimations of lucidity if one can pause long enough to listen.

When a human whispers, what they are actually doing is making a barely audible sound with little or no vibration of their vocal cords. A visual equivalent is entering a pool of water so slowly as to create virtually no discernible ripples, or walking in a wild space and leaving no trace of a broken organic element or visible footprint.

This morning, accompanied by this inquiry, I passed in front of the hibiscus, whose blooms were still cuddled in their morning huddle. I thought whimsically that the hibiscus was whispering into its soon to be shouting riotous color and unapologetic big beauty. To breathe in the whispers is to quietly take something in or to gently accept the truth of a tender situation.

Jeanette Richardson Herring shares, *"Pausing to breathe— taking in the softness, quietly listening to the secret whispers of life, ancestors, God. Breathe in, taking in fully with my complete attention that which is just under the surface layer of everyday noise. Pausing to do this is an act of the will to feed the soul."*

Lynda Allen explores these ideas in this way: *"For me, the key is the word pursuing. That feels like a pushing word, and when I feel like I'm pushing something rather than walking forward with it, I need to pause and look at why I'm pushing."*

Sharon Martinelli acknowledges that one of her favorite tools is the Pause button.

Caren Albers expands, *"I like the idea of pausing and resting, without judgement. Our culture often seems overly focused on starting and finishing. There is so much in the madcap middle not to be missed; so much relating, reliving, reconsidering, remaking, that the pause provides. Your not-yet-completed projects are not abandoned. They are in the fabulous phase of what and who they will become in their own time."*

Pausing or stopping pursuit of a thing is not a failure, it's a viable decision. To apply this question to something in your life, when you imagine not pursuing a thing for a time, do you feel remorse or relief? Is there regret at stopping, if only in your mental exploration? That can be an invitation to keep on with the pursuit. If, however, relief is your response at the thought of stopping, then a stop may be in order. A stop is not necessarily a conclusion, it is a pause. It provides time for refreshing the perspective and for reconsideration. You may have said you would do the thing. And you may very well still do it, just in a different context or timeframe then was initially planned. A pause gives time to evaluate whether the pause is temporary or permanent.

Katie Howard frequently asks her clients as well as herself, "Will taking a break help?"

"I don't care how long it takes, I'm sitting here until I fix this."

"You can just stay at the table until you finish this meal."

"I'll stay up all night if I have to get these done."

If you have ever said anything that sounds like these or heard them said, there is your proof that the benefit of taking a break has been overlooked. A dear person in my life who was in the grips of undiagnosed conditions would resolve any long frustration by unleashing a series of bloodcurdling screams. I was expressing sympathy for those within earshot when I realized that I identified with the practice. I confessed to my friend, a psychologist with whom I was traveling, that I would do a thing that I had learned in childhood from my constant companion, Pete, a Labrador Retriever. Then and now, when I reach a level of untenable frustration, I growl. Audibly I offer a series of grrrrr's that compete with the most astute warning from a guard dog. And then? I move on. My friend said that this is a fundamental reset button that applies both to animals and human beings. It is essentially a neurological release valve that allows the brain to disrupt the frustration pattern and start a new thought and thinking sequence. It's the same reason some say swearing is effective. Others steer away from the audible and suggest movement accomplishes the same thing. Movement! Busting a few dance moves, going for a walk, striking a yoga pose or two—all these create a break in an undesirable or seemingly unbreakable pattern. Intuitively, I leaned toward twenty- and forty-minute work blocks, beginning in grade school, and would take a hard stop from one activity and do something else for a while. Outside observers offered uninvited observations that perhaps I had attention deficit disorder. In practice, I was acting out of the most productive mechanism for completing a variety of tasks. In recent years, this has been dubbed the Pomodoro method because of the tomato-shaped kitchen timer that its originator, Francesco Cirillo, utilized to set specific blocks of time dedicated to a single task before taking a break. This method is helpful to me when I am doing something that I don't especially like. By contrast, when I am in flow, four hours can actually feel like forty minutes. Breaking tasks into small blocks of time actually can increase productivity and innovation and can lead to previously unavailable or not-yet-imagined solutions.

When you are stuck in the loop of a seemingly unsolvable problem, hear this: "Walk away. Just walk away." Yes, walk away and return later with fresh eyes. A friend thought she hated a major project she'd just finished. She walked away, slept on it without taking any action in her phase of hating the entire project and feeling like throwing it all away. But upon waking, she knew exactly what it was. Two major elements had inadvertently been left out of the entire endeavor. She didn't actually hate it, she simply had experienced extreme discomfort that it didn't feel right. The break allowed her the capacity to consider differently and discover was what was at the heart of her strong reaction.

I took some training in Aikido, which laid a foundation for learning the power of doing nothing. The meaning of "taking no action in this moment" can be expressed in a single familiar word: Pause. Decades ago, I was a consummate do-er. I believed that everything merited an action or a response. You've heard it said or perhaps you've said it yourself, "Well, I can't just stand around and do nothing." Turns out, you can. It's not always the best option, but sometimes it is.

Certain instances immediately come to mind. In one recollection, I acted immediately, and my action was followed by weeks of anxiety and ridiculous what-if-ing. If only I had paused and done nothing, the force of organic circumstances would have resolved the issue without any intervention from me, as it finally did. I acted when I could have paused. In another instance in which I had very strong feelings about actions that directly impacted me, I selected the pause as my best response. After a few weeks of silence, the individual resolved the circumstance precisely as I'd hoped—all on their own. It was my "doing nothing" that allowed them the space to come to a conclusion that was both kind and fair.

As Caren Albers explores, *"Waiting, like pausing, is an action. When we jump in to solve our children's, relative's, or friend's problems, we can do more harm than good. Not doing so empowers people to solve their own problems; and by jumping in, we disempower them. Yes—pausing, waiting, can be difficult but is a great lesson. Fixing something for others often just 'kicks the can down the road.' By not always stepping in, they 'learn how to fish.'"*

The consequence of not acting can be disastrous. When one does not pay attention to the signs of progressing illness or when you or someone else are in imminent danger are two examples of this. The pause, an *un*action, is a viable tool in a decision tool kit. Turns out doing nothing *is* doing something.

How might you employ the practice of a long pause or purposeful inaction today?

184 | "No" is a complete sentence, and every upside has a downside.

It's more of a question than a statement: Everything that is desirable has a downside. The potential for negative impact exists within almost anything, maybe everything. This may relate to that old adage, "One man's medicine is another man's poison." Does this mean your perspective of an upside could in fact be my downside? Yep.

While the opportunity to engage in brief conversations with dozens of different people over a two-hour period of time is an upside for an extrovert, it is a decided downside for an introvert. I can learn from my friend, coworker, or family member to graciously accommodate that any downside might be an upside for another. There are people in the world whose job is to identify the downside of anything: strategists, extraordinary event managers, and engineers. They keep us safe and in ease by looking at a plan and seeing the drawbacks, potential pitfalls, negative elements, and systemic weaknesses. People committed to chronic positivity may be tempted to categorize this population as naysayers. Yet considering the downside of most anything allows a strategy or a plan to be complete and multifaceted. In specific instances, it means that an individual is better prepared in case things do not unfold as positively intended. In that circumstance, those considered naysayers become the only ones able to deliver an unreserved "yes!" to the unexpected circumstance.

Perhaps I will start calling it looking at a thing from another side rather than identifying it specifically as a downside. Because I think I've proved to myself that down can become up in a hot minute.

Is there a downside to imagining you've said *No*?
How's it feel?

185 | *There are things that serve more broadly when they are released.*

Release. Free. Let go. Liberate. Emancipate.

Release is an action that can be taken by someone else on your behalf or experienced at a wholly personal level, initiated on your own behalf by you!

It takes a great effort to hold onto a thing over a period of time. A clenched fist becomes uncomfortable, even painful, before much time has passed. Release implies an unfetteredness. The braces released by a falconer allow the hawk to see; the release of the halsband lets a falcon fly freely. The bindings used in falconry are a matter of training and discipline. In human experience, much of the things which are bound or carried are inadvertent, unconscious, and often accidental. An arrow with weights attached will not position easily at its nock or go very far or with any level of accuracy. Once an arrow is unburdened, it fits easily onto the bowstring and can be released with precision and strength in the pull. What a metaphor for personal momentum when that which is tied and hauled about is set free, let go, released.

Letting go of expectations allows every (new) experience to stand on its own merit, and even some old ones. This seems really appropriate for entertainment events, meeting someone new, having a spontaneous date night with a long-time partner; any interaction where you and another are meeting by agreement in a field, an equal playing field. I do not hold this as an ideal directive in all situations. When a person or institution identifies a set of expectations that they invite you to have? Have them. Go ahead—confidently have them and hold to them. And provide accountability with grace or graciousness when the expectations that were outlined for you to anticipate were not matched. Some endeavors have a greater sense of discovery if expectations are completely dismissed. Scientific research is a good example of this. I've repeated, "We see what we expect to see." That's bias. Letting go of expectation allows a scientist to see what is actually there, not what they anticipate will be there. In other situations, when you pay for a service, it's advisable to hold to account or fulfillment what you are told you may reasonably expect. If you purchased a ticket and expected a breed-specific dog show and you showed up to discover a deplorable backstreet-style dogfight, you would want a refund at the very least. Were dogs involved? Yes indeed, but not the expectations that you were sold and told you could expect.

What will you let go of?

186 | *Rest for a moment on the strength of your choices.*

We hear the sequential call in lines from stores to banks to clinical waiting rooms: "Next!" To rest even for a moment in the strength of a choice is not common in our culture. The rapid pace of our society, which can border on an almost hysterical speed, itself demands, "Next," like a drill sergeant barking out the command, "Move it!" Reflection and contemplation, rest and savoring, are not components you often see built into an organizational plan. Perhaps at the end of a project an emotionally intelligent executive will build in a "celebrate the success" moment. Even in that, it is only a pause before the team moves on to their next set of choices. I once wrote out the question,

"Of what is my life built, if not a series of considered choices?" An impactful learning opportunity is overlooked by not resting in the strength of all the choices that lead you to an ultimate conclusion. At least this rest, this pause, can be a consideration for some of the more significant decisions and choices that you embrace in your day.

When I allow Webster, my rat terrier pal, to depend on remembering all his good habits formed with former consistent training without reinforcing those behaviors, he begins to let them go. He moves into disregarding or forgetting, as if the previously habitual action has become brand-new and is being done for the very first time. So when he comes the first time I call him, I turn it into an Olympic gold moment. With that kind of praise, he is more likely to remember next time. Who would want to willingly pass up an Olympic gold praise moment? Even the most humble among us appreciate their strengths being noticed, even celebrated. Resting on the strength of a choice turns it into your Olympic gold moment.

Psychologists and other mental health professionals assess the reality of "decision fatigue." The choices we make every day can run into the thousands, from the subtle (cream, half-and-half, milk?) to the clearly significant (say yes to the promotion?). Roy F. Baumeister, a social psychologist, first coined the phrase. It's increasingly known that the quality of choices diminish as their required number increases. Resting even for a short period on the strength of a choice is a small reset button—a sanctuary moment on the slog of the long journey of key daily choices. Such a pause teaches about what you did well and gives you a map so that you can purposely repeat it. Getting that sweet recognition of "Good job!" delivered to your soul reinforces whatever it was you decided. Savoring a gold medal moment for your own strong choice allows you not only to repeat it but to recognize it and even see the opportunity to use it again, well before the next time happens.

Steve Jobs famously wore the same style of clothes every day because he wanted to reserve his decision-making capacity for things that were of a greater consequence to him than his attire. So when he showed up in his jeans and black turtleneck, you knew that the energy required for him to put those clothes on that particular day was minimal. In my own environment, I am aware of the opportunity to reduce my own fatigue in making decisions by purposely limiting them. Perhaps you have heard that the more choices a shopper is given for a single type of product, the less likely they are to even make a choice. A new parent is taught to work with a toddler by either offering no choice, "Today we get to enjoy a toasted cheese sandwich for lunch," or the two-choice "this or that" model. It is easier to make a choice between two things than it is to make a choice between seven things. This is very true for humans early in their developmental stage, like toddlers. It also happens to be true for adults, at any age.

Rest up! Enjoy the strength of a particular decision that you have just made. See it for what it is. This is not only helpful to you both in the moment and with future similar decisions but gives you the opportunity to share the process with another and perhaps support or lead them into the strength of their own excellent, gold medal choice.

What choice of yours will you revel in and rest in today?

Nature provides an ideal model for shedding and letting go.

In a colder season, a dog prepares with a thicker coat to better govern body temperature. A healthy dog sheds the undercoat to make room for new growth when spring comes around.

Trees shed their leaves to most appropriately direct their core vitality to maintain their own life force rather than disseminating their energy to maintain their fragile leaf system in the coldest season of the year.

Humans shed hundreds of thousands of skin particles every hour—in every season! The skin is the largest organ, and shedding is a process essential to a healthy body. Absent the healthy shedding process, medical conditions occur ranging from a simply irritated skin surface to forms of ichthyosis, a condition that impacts the rate at which the skin regenerates.

In natural models, it is easy to identify the benefits of shedding. They translate metaphorically to improved practices:

- Shedding outdated ideas provides space for growth.
- Shedding unnecessary protocols allows energy be to be directed more specifically to essential components.
- Shedding appropriate bits allows for a cycle of health and vitality.

What can you shed today?

What must I first finish before I can start on this?

Some things are better done (and done better) in sequence, and some things *must* be done in sequence. And some tasks and processes can be randomly selected for action, while there are other things that are enjoyable when done somewhat concurrently. I relish the opportunity to work on several different pieces of writing—different projects, each with a distinct voice. Reading a few different books in the same period of time is something I like to do. Yet gas must be put in the tank before the car will operate on its own. Or an electric car must first be charged to have any get-up-and-go!

I noticed something when helping a friend prepare to leave the country for an extended time. We had to get her belongings to her storage unit, there was paperwork to complete and mail to be forwarded, and she needed to pack her suitcases, all before I could take her to the airport. The case could have been made that her belongings could have been abandoned and she could just go get on the plane with only her ticket and passport. The consequences of those actions are generally undesirable. Certain things had to be finished before she could enjoy the start of her journey.

Understanding the sequence of finishes and starts is a keen dividing element in some relationships. Order/chaos; one thing at a time vs. many things at a time; these two ways of approaching decisions, choices, and systems are largely a matter of preference and personality. And they ultimately work in the context of each

Courage Doesn't Always Roar...

individual's way of doing and being. Still, there remain some core things that simply must be done in a sequence: First this, then that. Understanding the *must* of this allows a clear priority to rise.

What can you finish that will make room for a beginning?

189 | *Balance does not occur in the specific but in the whole.*

I like the phrase, "in the whole." I precede certain observations with, "overall…" or, "on balance…"

These are the phrases where I refer to balance. Rarely can I identify a pristine division of percentages effectively measuring anything. Equilibrium manifests in the aggregate, not the individual specifics. Individuals seeking a consistent 50/50 split in any event are headed for various frustrations. 80/20, 70/30, 60/40, 50/50… These are the percentages that end up creating an ultimate balancing act. Is an eighteen-hour workday balanced? Not on that specific day, certainly. In a work week that is followed by many delightful play days, it takes on a wonderful balance.

Look for balance in the whole.

The concept of wholeness has been elusive. I've tried to define it over the years. There are many ways I can say how I know it is not. Perhaps wholeness is defined or articulated differently, uniquely, in various phases of life and for each individual.

My body delivers distinct messages to me when I step away from a sense of wholeness. I bump into things, and I'll make the joke, "Hey! who moved the door jamb?" I trip, I fall. So by looking at what it is not, I can say a sense of wholeness has an uprightness to it, a balance. I find it difficult to complete things or make decisions when I am away from my own sense of wholeness. Wholeness doesn't seem to have as much to do with comfort as much as it does ease and flow. The discomfort of change is part of a whole and dynamic life, yet that isn't especially comfortable as a condition! Perhaps wholeness has more to do with congruence, integration, when the elements of a moment, event, day, or life are matched, mirrored with consciously held intentions. This essential alignment brings a unifying momentum, a confidence to decisions and actions. It is not defined by what is convenient or manageable but rather by how I am able to manage whatever comes my way. It is this balance between my inside condition and outside actions and attitudes that creates and comprises my sense of wholeness at any given time. This means that even in deficit, grief, unwellness, or challenge, I can indeed experience a sense of balance and wholeness.

Where is it you find your sense of wholeness and balance?

Afterword

A Love Letter To Courage

Dear capricious, consistent, contradictory courage,
Please greet your family for me.
Clarity, compassion and consistency are such fine siblings.
I know you each have compelling work to do.
I'm sure you all wish you could
gather together more often. Just for fun.
You are all fully occupied answering
the call for the greater good.
I admire that about you.
No call for help is too small.
You manage to hear the quietest whisper for assistance.
You're so good that way. I'm grateful
for all the ways you've shown up for me.
My earliest recollections of your presence are with me
always, they are among my guiding principles.
Navigating the dangerous structures built of
alcoholism required you by my side.
I know that choosing to hide from inevitable abuse
didn't look brave to others,
but you and I knew it was my
most autonomous and courageous choice.
And when I grew up enough, was I eight?

you were right there with me,
holding high my clenched fists and
giving breath to strengthen my voice.
Never. Ever. Do. That. Again. NEVER.
Just as you promised it would, that courageous stand
worked. You taught me how to use my voice
for myself as well as in the service of others.
Courage, you wear so many different hats and
garments that people don't always recognize you.
Even I am sometimes unable to see that it is you.
Ah, but when you speak I recognize you immediately.
You provide different directions and
some of them seem contradictory in nature.
Go here.
Choose another way.
Wait: time will tend this, not you.
This one is yours to carry, pick it up.
Let go of your end of the rope, now.
This is not yours.
Try that road and see where it goes.
Pack light, it's a long road ahead.
I'm grateful for the thousands of times
you have whispered to me,
"stop for now. Try again tomorrow."

Love,
Mary Anne Em Radmacher

Acknowledgements

The iDecide365 subscriber learning community provides support in so many ways. They invest their resources in my daily writing. They willingly engage in a dynamic learning community. They forge trusted bonds and share and anchor the learning with each other. In this process I am writer, facilitator, and student of dozens of amazing people. All of the participation in this group is valued and valuable. There were some comments so relevant to what I wrote that I asked their permission to include them here.

With appreciation, I acknowledge the generous contributions of:

Candace Doby, speaker and author; Barbara Grassey, business consultant; Paula Rudberg Lowe, editor, publisher, and community activist; Pat Weiderspan Jones, teacher and artist; Kirstin Bolander Rich, administrator; Lynda Allen, poet and artist; Kim Jayhan Pique, author; Dr. Susan Paul Johnson, expressive arts instructor; Jeanette Richardson Herring, author and artist; Brandie Sellers, therapist; Cheryl Craigie, retired CEO and creative seeker; Caren Albers, author and poet; Leonore Curren, dancer; Connie Bennett, playwright; Beverly Kipp, nurse and lay minister; Maxine Rothman, weaver and spinner; Susan Knezel Reardon, educator and poet; Paul Wesselmann, speaker and author; Sue Robson, jeweler and lay minister; Liz Amaya-Fernandez, doula, educator, and poet; Jean Robin Martell, photographer; Heather M. Mack, collaborative minister; Dr. Martina

McGowan, poet and retired physician; Kathleen Everett, nurse and advice columnist; and Sharon Martinelli, CPA and coach.

The members of iDecide365 who actively participated and have not been directly quoted include:

Jane Vader, who represented concepts visually every day and inspired us; Pam Matchie-Thiede; Susan Woodall Lane; Elizabeth Drewry Beck; Dr. Deanna Davis; Pam Williams; Debbie Mackie; Jayne Edgington; Susan Lucas; Alison Campbell; Shawn Patrick Rivera; Di Bagley; Lynda Irvin; Jeanne Johnson; Linda Bannen; Robbie Zumajit Hanson; Robert Ruder; Kathleen Pizzello; Dr. Kymn Harvin; Marcey Langworthy Balcomb; Mary Gurney; Ann Bell; Katie Locke; Frances Accuntius-Stone; Tami Dillon; Francis Olson; Elizabeth Crouch; Mary Meares; Jo Ann Coignet; and Jean Pirkl.

These lifelong learners have enriched my personal life and helped me become a better writer and communicator. It's been a privilege to keep daily company with them.

The fine staff at Mango Publishing have helped at every level; to Brenda Knight, a visionary who has long and tirelessly believed in my work in the world, thank you for welcoming me into your community of authors.

Authors do not write in a vacuum. I share beautiful space with two fine souls who adore dogs as much as I do and whose enthusiasm for them and for sun gets me outdoors more than my hermit ways would normally allow.

Sharon Martinelli, Pam Matchie-Thiede, and Caren Albers, who say yes to any journey I undertake, thank you. Thanks to: J.D.

Hildebrand, who doesn't appear in these pages but whose presence has been improving my practices for a few decades; Candace Doby for reaching out to me so many years ago and giving me the thrill of watching you shine; Akasia, Kathy, Sandra, and Jeanette, who helped me feel as if I were writing a love letter every day for a year. In fact, much of this book feels like a love letter—one addressed to you, the reader. Not fancy or flowery but accompanied with the wish that I inspire you to acknowledge all the ways you courageously show up in the world.

My thanks to Margo Dueber, who prompted this courage poem, and Paul Dueber, who gave me my first set of professional markers. I appreciate the long roads we share.

I have love and gratitude for the people mentioned here and so much fondness for so many who are not listed.

About the Author

Mary Anne Em Radmacher is an inspiring and prolific writer, poet, aphorist, and artist. She delivers a powerful keynote and training session as well. Every aspect of her life, both personal and professional, is creative. Her works travel the globe; among the most famous is: *Courage Doesn't Always Roar. Sometimes courage is the quiet voice at the end of the day saying, "I will try again tomorrow."*

Her quote, "I am not the same having seen the moon shine on the other side of the world," is featured on foreign exchange student web sites around the world and used by those who understand the true nature of travel.

She's been making meaning out of her life through her personal practice since she was in second grade. That commitment to writing produced a lifelong curiosity for learning both about the inner and outer world. She is the author of over a dozen books, including *Lean Forward Into Your Life*, *Live With Intention*, and first in her iDecide365 series, *Live Your Best Story*. Each of her books is loaded with relevant content from her insights and the experiences of her lifetime, and in *Live With Intention*, she shares one of her signature programs, "Remember and Do What Matters." In addition to classes and group coaching, which she calls "MindHive," she reaches for ever invigorating wellness practices and insists life is better when accompanied by Dog. She's especially fond of lemon squares as an occasional treat.

She flexibly practices the ability to mindfully move in all ways from outmoded practices to habitats to moving her body. She treasures the opportunity to travel to new places and loves to return home.

You can connect with her through her web site at:

maryanneradmacher.net

Mango Publishing, established in 2014, publishes an eclectic list of books by diverse authors—both new and established voices—on topics ranging from business, personal growth, women's empowerment, LGBTQ studies, health, and spirituality to history, popular culture, time management, decluttering, lifestyle, mental wellness, aging, and sustainable living. We were recently named 2019 *and* 2020's #1 fastest-growing independent publisher by *Publishers Weekly*. Our success is driven by our main goal, which is to publish high-quality books that will entertain readers as well as make a positive difference in their lives.

Our readers are our most important resource; we value your input, suggestions, and ideas. We'd love to hear from you—after all, we are publishing books for you!

Please stay in touch with us and follow us at:

Facebook: Mango Publishing

Twitter: @MangoPublishing

Instagram: @MangoPublishing

LinkedIn: Mango Publishing

Pinterest: Mango Publishing

Newsletter: mangopublishinggroup.com/newsletter

Join us on Mango's journey to reinvent publishing, one book at a time.